A Day at

by

Steve Kirby

RB
Rossendale Books

Published by Lulu Enterprises Inc.
3101 Hillsborough Street
Suite 210
Raleigh, NC 27607–5436
United States of America

Published in paperback 2018
Category: Sports
Copyright Steve Kirby © 2018
ISBN : 978-0-244-37395-5

All rights reserved, Copyright under Berne Copyright Convention and Pan American Convention. No part of this book may be reproduced, stored in a retrieval system, or transmitted in any form or by any means, electronic, mechanical, photocopying, recording or otherwise, without prior permission of the author. The author's moral rights have been asserted.

About the Author

Steve Kirby was born on May 28th, 1971 and comes from a small East Devon Village that no–one has ever heard of. He studied as a Civil Engineer at Exeter progressing as an Incorporated Engineer at the Institution of Civil Engineers, London.

Steve has worked as a highway design engineer for various highway authorities and council offices throughout the south west of England. He considered writing a book about his experience of working for local government but decided that nobody would believe a word of it.

Out–side of work, Steve Kirby holds a passion for time trialling and still competes. Even at his age! As well as competing he is a devoted race secretary for his Plymouth based team, 'City Cycle Couriers', and enjoys helping and encouraging others to become involved with the sport. The purpose of this short story is to do just that and to explain why the dark art of time trialling has been so successful since its birth, way back in 1895.

CONTENTS

Foreword 7

Prologue 9

TT Talk – A Glossary 12

What's It All About? 21

Flamme Rouge – A Day At the Races 30

Arrivée 83

Lantern Rouge – A Beginner's Guide 88

Getting Started 95

Training 113

UK Competition Records 147

World Hour Records 150

Foreword

It is 5am on a warm June morning. It's just becoming light and the dawn chorus is in full swing. The event secretary is approaching the village hall avoiding the newly fledged wrens, sparrows, song thrushes and blackbirds that are dashing in and out of the hedgerows and leading him up to the hall. The already tired volunteer now fumbles with unfamiliar keys and attempts to unlock the slightly rotted door to the old crumbing hall which has seen better days. The Village Hall will, for the next 5 hours be the race headquarters for a Time Trial event. It is an event which he has meticulously planned over the last three months. The lock finally releases and to his relief the doors swing open. The little light there is immediately floods the dusty room...

Prologue

'*Ride your bike, ride your bike, ride your bike*', echoed the famous quote by the five–time Giro d Italia and two time Tour de France Winner, Fausto Coppi.
As quotes go this is not a bad one and quite possibly the most important piece of advice you could give to any aspiring time trialist or for any other type of competing cyclist for that matter.

This book however is not a guide, or a training program and it is not aimed at riders looking to gain more power to go faster in what many refer to as the 'dark side' of cycle racing. There are plenty of books already available for that sort of thing as well as a vast amount of material available on the internet. Although the best advice I could give in this arena would be to invest in a coach and take the guess work out. Such training books, bibles, programs etc can be misleading and not specific to you as an individual so we need to tread very carefully when considering generic training advice.

The objective of this book is to capture the essence of what it is like to become involved in the UK time-trialling scene.

The book essentially contains a short story describing a typical day at a UK Time-trial event. The story unfolds the day through the eyes of some of the people involved in TT including those of the event secretary, a marshal, a rider and a few other characters we pick up along the way. I hope that anyone already involved with UK TT will be able to relate to the characters one way or another. The story attempts to capture the true feel of a typical UK event including some of the quirky topics that this sport brings us.

Whilst this book is not a guide to time-trialling, the Lantern Rouge Chapter contains information about how to get involved and how to get started in the hobby. It attempts to describe why time-trialling might appeal to any beginner wishing to start racing and much advice is provided for those wishing to do so.

We end the book with a list of the UK TT records (Up to end 2017) and a potted history of the famous Hour Record.

For those who don't know, Coppi's era was 1940's early 50's so of course time–trialling has come a long way since then and found itself under the microscope in many ways. Some things have changed, but the fundamentals remain the same. Whilst equipment, training, sports science and all manner of things may have evolved it is still essentially about a person on a bike riding against a stopwatch. It is also simply about getting out on your bike so believe in Fausto...

Ride your bike, Ride your bike. Ride your bike!!

TT Talk – A Glossary

The following is a glossary of terms often heard in UK time–trialling together with their true meanings. Some are more obvious than others and some are just downright baffling to the uninitiated. So please use this as a reference as some of the abbreviations will be found throughout the book. They are in no particular order.

- **TT** – Time Trial

- **RR** – Road Race

- **TTT** – Team Time–Trial. Usually referred to as a 2up, 3up or 4up.

- **10, 25, 50, 100** – A number describing the distance in miles of the TT.

- **12hr, 24hr TT** – Ultra distance TT. Only attempted by those who wear their underwear on the outside of their skin suit.

- **Skin suit** – Repulsive, skin tight, all in one, aerodynamic garment worn by many TT riders, Wrestlers and Superheroes.

- **Sporting** – The term that refers to a rolling, hilly or sometimes torturous course. Usually on single carriageways with potholes, traffic, mud, and a road surface that will rattle your fillings out.

- **The start** – A position of no particular interest, miles away from the HQ. It might be described as 'The 8th lamp post after the cattle grid' or the third drain from a farm gate. It is sometimes an imaginary line on the edge of an extremely busy and dangerous Dual–Carriageway, accessed only by a mud covered, flooded and potholed farm track.

- **HQ** – A scout hut, primary school, community room, village hall, occasionally a lay–by in the middle of nowhere or if you are very lucky a pub, will be the location of the Headquarters (HQ). It is a place for gathering with fellow racers, a place to provide excuses for your piss poor performance or the place to gorge yourself with cake and be smug when you have beaten all your mates. It is occasionally the place to throw your aero helmet across the room in anger after a DNF, a place to throw your toys out of the pram and argue with the organiser and a place to storm out of before driving off like a lunatic sobbing, after leaving your disc leaning against the boot of your car.

- **DNF** – Did Not Finish.

- **DNS** – Did Not Start.

- **DQ** – Disqualified.

- **Aero helmet** – Strange pointy helmet resembling the silhouette of the character in the classic Ridley Scott Movie 'Alien'.

- **Disc** – Solid Carbon Fibre rear wheel that makes your bike sound like an approaching Star Wars TIE Fighter.

- **Over socks** – Lycra socks like 'Super Heroes' and 'American Wrestlers' often wear. They slip over your shoes to help with aerodynamics, but the jury is still out there whether they do anything other than make you look a bit silly.

- **Tub** – Sometimes referred to as 'Tubular' and preferred by many TT riders. A tyre without an inner tube that is glued onto the wheel rim and can withstand very high pressure.

- **Clincher** – A traditional type of tyre found on most commercially sold bikes. It is attached to a hooked rim by a bead and has an inner tube. This is preferred for general riding and training as roadside punctures are easier to repair.

- **HRM** – Heart rate monitor. Often a function of the bike computer and records heart rate in beats per minute. (bpm)

- **Turbo trainer** – An instrument of torture which clamps your bike to a resistance unit by the back wheel enabling you to train in your garage, shed, spare room or even the bedroom! It should be the first thing you rescue if your house is on fire and quite possibly the most important piece of your training armoury.

- **FTP** – Functional Threshold Power.

- **BAR** – Best All Round. A term used for a regional league table to identify the best all round tester in that region. Often measured by way of average speed over a mix of distances.

- **Cadence** – The term used for the speed of pedalling in revolutions per minute (rpm)

- **The turn** – Another position of no particular interest, often a roundabout or motorway junction where bored looking marshals, will direct you back to where you came from.

- **Marshal** – A person who has selflessly given up their Sunday morning to get bored watching 50 odd time–trial riders pass them. Without these volunteers there would be no TT so please spare a thought and if you can spare a breath at the turn, perhaps a 'thank you' as well?

- **Timekeeper** – The lady or gentleman at the finish who is there to ensure that you miss your PB by 1 second. Like the marshal the timekeeper has also volunteered to give up half their weekend in order to make YOUR race possible. Please acknowledge these volunteers if you are a rider.

- **PB** – Personal Best. The best time you set for that distance or course. If you miss the PB by a single second, return to the HQ and throw aero helmet across the room.

- **Pusher Off** – Usually an experienced rider who will hold each rider up at the start so that the rider may clip into the pedals. Not essential but seen at most Open Events.

- **Event Secretary** – The lady or gentleman at the HQ who has given up half their life to organise the event from scratch. He or she is the key contact whose details are listed within the handbook published by the CTT.

- **Long xx** – Where xx is the number of minutes in your resulting TT time. For example, if you record

21:55 for a ten–mile TT, it could be called a long 21.

- **Short xx** – Work it out.

- **00 man or woman** – A seeded rider. Normally fast who gets to wear a 0 number such as 50, 40, 30, and 20. These guys (or girls) are likely to pass you and are identifiable only by a sound not dissimilar to a Star Wars TIE fighter.

- **05 man or woman** – Also a seeded rider. Not as fast as a 00 but will wear numbers 45, 35, 25 etc. All the other numbers are filled by riders who have a life.

- **Minute man** – The man or woman who sets off one minute before you. Experienced riders will ignore this person. Less experienced will tear off like a lunatic in order to catch the minute man. Then fade away and record a time slower than that of their PB. They might throw their aero helmet across the HQ.

- **2–minute man** – Work it out.

- **Tester** – A slang word for time–trial rider.

- **CTT** – The National Governing body for 'Cycling Time Trials' in England and Wales

- **BC** – (British Cycling). The recognised governing body for cycle sport in the UK.

- **UCI** – (Union Cycliste Internationale). The World governing body for Cycle Sport.

- **The Handbook** – A book which can be purchased from the CTT. It contains rules, regulations, details of open events, past & current champions and much more.

- **Open event** – Formal events which attract riders from any UK club that is registered with the CTT. There will be a closing date around a couple of weeks prior to the event.

- **Club event** – Less formal than open events. Typically held mid–week by a cycling club and can be entered on the night. They are usually open to riders outside of the club but dominated by the club's own members.

- **Depart** – French word for the start of a race.

- **Arrivée** – French word for the end of a race.

- **Chequered board** – The grey blurred thing at the 'Finish'. It is a chequered flag to signify the end of your race and usually leaning against the wheel arch of the time keeper's car. It is a beautiful sight at first, but it very cruelly seems to take forever to reach.

- **The Finish** – The finish is marked by the chequered board and a grinning timekeeper. Please don't be disappointed if there is no over the road banner saying 'Arrivee', or if there is no euro pop band, no champagne, no celebrity, no podium and no dancing girls. The finish is unfortunately likely to be in the middle of nowhere and miles away from the HQ which is your next destination. If you are very lucky there may be a bit of cake left and plenty of people to see you throw your aero helmet across the room.

What's It All About?

It is popular belief that the French invented cycle racing and that the first ever bicycle race was held on 31st May 1868 over a 1.2km course at The Parc de Saint–Cloud, Paris. Ok the road racers among you might wish to add that it was in fact an Englishman named James Moore who was the victor of that first ever bicycle race.

So, France takes the credit for inventing cycle racing. But it is in fact the British who invented the sport we know as Time–Trialling. That's right TT was born in the UK due to a burning desire within cyclists of the age to continue to race when mass start races were banned in the late 1800's. *It was banned because it scared the horses! Perhaps this is why bunch racing excelled in France, as the French are perhaps less sympathetic to horses than we are in the UK?*

In order not to scare horses or make work for the local Bobby, a rebel organisation was formed under the influence of men such as Frederick Thomas Bidlake, to continue racing on the road without attracting police attention. These groups would organise secret meets and cunningly set off at one–minute intervals. They would be discreetly racing against the clock, whilst pretending to go about their normal business.

Time–trialling could therefore be compared to other eccentric British sports such as Cheese Rolling, Gurning, Bog Snorkelling and Shin Kicking. Although I like to think that TT is probably more painful than at least three of the above.

There is a dispute over which was the first ever TT, but the credit is generally given to Bidlake's North Road Cycling Club of London. If that is correct, the first ever TT was held on 5th October 1895 and covered a distance of 50 miles. The North Road CC, continue to thrive as a club today.

Ok, so the British invented this sport so naturally like other sports we invent, we must be pretty terrible at it right? Wrong!

Many of the world's best time trial riders have in fact come from the UK. I don't just mean following the success of Bradley Wiggins and Chris Froome at the Tour de France, nor do I mean Bradley's Olympic glory at London 2012 and his World title of 2014, but for many decades British riders have excelled throughout the world in TT. Here are just a few of those examples: –

- **Ray Booty** – It is historically recorded that in 1954, Roger Bannister was famed for being the first runner to break the four–minute mile and an event which became one of the most iconic sporting moments in history. Two years later, there were fewer headlines when Ray Booty became the first cyclist to break four hours in a 100–mile TT with a time of 3:58:28. Although this was arguably iconic as Bannister's four–minute mile, it was never recognised as such. It didn't really help that cycling was still sporting backwater at the time and was almost an undercover sport in Britain following its earlier ban. (Remember the horses). However, word of Booty's achievement had caused quite a stir in France and it seemed to be a world record at that time. In September of the same year, Booty also smashed the 'straight out' 100–mile record with a time of 3:28:40. A record which stood for 34 years.

- **Graeme Obree** – Also known as 'The Flying Scotsman' was a pure 'Tester' who in 1993 broke the world hour record. He was noted for breaking such record on a homemade bike made from BMX and washing machine parts. It also had very unusual riding position. Obree pet named the bike, 'Old Faithfull'. His hour record lasted for less than a week when Englishman, Chris Boardman broke it by 674 metres. Obree returned in 1994 after a few tweaks to 'Old Faithfull' to break Boardman's record and setting a new mark of 52.713km. This time using the same velodrome that Boardman had used in Bordeaux. But just 3 months later his record fell once again, this time to Miguel Indurain of Spain. The UCI grew concerned that changes to the bicycles were responsible for the sudden increase in speeds and so banned such practices and subsequently de–recognised these 'World Hour Records'. As well as breaking records, Obree was also World 4000m Pursuit champion in 1993 & 1995.

- **Chris Boardman MBE** – Olympic medallist, hour record breaker, yellow jersey holder and multi world champion on the track. Boardman left no stone unturned in his quest for speed and his palmares are just too long to list here. With his specialism in TT and track racing, one of his major achievements include his Tour de France prologue win in 1994, which at a speed of 55.152km/h remained the fastest stage of any Grand Tour for 21 years. Boardman also broke the world hour record in the famous battle of the 90's with Graeme Obree. Having those records de-recognised by the UCI, Boardman went on to break the 'UCI Hour' in 2000, which was basically the same thing but introduced by the UCI to ensure that the bikes used resembled the Bike used by Eddy Merckx in the 1970's. He only beat Merckx's record by 10 metres, but it was the new mark nonetheless at 49.441km.

- **David Millar** – Multiple Tour de France stage winner Millar still holds a Tour de France record in TT. Whilst Chris Boardman held the record for the fastest ever TT in a Tour de France, it was over a distance of just 7.1km. In 2003, Millar won the 49km TT stage in Nantes which is still the fastest ever tour stage over a distance greater than 25km. He also won the prologue TT in 2000 and the Commonwealth Games TT in 2010. Millar was stripped of some of his achievements including his rainbow jersey and gold medal at the Worlds TT following the discovery of performance enhancing drugs in his flat. He became very open about his doping and welcomed his ban and subsequent stripping of many achievements but returned to the sport after the ban and even won two further Tour de France stages. The first was the 2011 TTT and the second was stage 12 of the 2012 edition giving him a total of 4 Tour de France stage wins.

- **Sir Bradley Wiggins** – Following his victory at the Tour de France in 2012, Wiggins is arguably Britain's most successful cyclist. He started his professional racing career on the track and won a bronze medal at the 2000 Olympic Games in Sydney. At the 2004 games in Athens, he took gold in the 4km individual pursuit, silver in the team pursuit and bronze in the Madison. At the 2008 summer games he contributed heavily to the

'Great Haul of China', taking gold again in the 4km individual pursuit and further gold in the team event, smashing a world record in the process. At the 2012 Games on home soil, Wiggins switched his focus to the road and won gold in the TT. Wiggins also took numerous victories at the UCI World track championships spanning a period of 14 years. It was 2012 though which was Bradley's year when he won the Tour de France including both of the TT stages. In the same year he won Paris Nice, Tour of Romandy as well as the Criterium de Dauphine winning all the TT stages in those major world stage events. Not only was Wiggins the first British rider to win the Tour de France but he is the only rider ever to win an Olympic gold medal in the same year. Just two years later at the 2014 Worlds, he added World Champion in the TT to his palmarès, possibly his greatest TT achievement over an amazing career. It does not end there though because Wiggins went on to break the hour record in 2015 with a new unified distance of 54.526km. Now, how does anyone follow that?

This is how...

➢ **Beryl Burton OBE** – I have deliberately saved the best for last. Wiggins may shine bright on the World stage, but Burton was arguably not only the best TT rider that Great Britain ever produced, but quite possibly the best all round cyclist the world has ever seen. Beryl Burton was the 'Yorkshire Flyer' and remains even after her death in 1996, the most prolific champion winner of all time with a tally of titles that not even the great Eddy Merckx could rival. With a career spanning over a quarter of a century she won no less than 122 British National Championships and reigned Women's British Best All Rounder for an unbroken 25–year sequence between 1959 and 1984. Burton was not only a formidable TT rider, but she also took the spotlight on the World stage winning an incredible seven rainbow jerseys on road and track.

The mark of Burton's brilliance was also noted in 1967 when she broke the British National 12–hour TT record. On that day the British TT Champion Mike McNamara started as favourite and was on his way to breaking the 9–year–old record with a distance of 276.5 miles. It was looking like a sure thing for McNamara. That is until Burton, who started 2 minutes behind him, not only caught her two–minute man but offered him a liquorice as she sailed past. He respectfully accepted the sweet and subsequent defeat before she then powered on to smash the **Men's** record by a further 6 miles! Now that's incredible.

Flamme Rouge – A Day At the Races

It is 5am on a warm June morning. It's just becoming light and the dawn chorus is in full swing. The event secretary is approaching the village hall avoiding the newly fledged wrens, sparrows, song thrushes and blackbirds that are dashing in and out of the hedgerows and leading him up to the hall. The already tired volunteer now fumbles with unfamiliar keys and attempts to unlock the slightly rotted door to the old crumbing hall which has seen better days. The Village Hall will, for the next 5 hours be the race HQ for a TT event. A TT event he has planned meticulously for the last three months. The lock finally releases and to his relief the doors swing open. The little light there is immediately floods the dusty room.

* * *

If I was to sum up the United Kingdom TT scene in one line, it would be this: *'Unspoilt by Money'*.

On the continent in countries such as France, Belgium and Italy, thousands of spectators line the roads in anticipation of the approaching peloton. There would be dozens of police escort vehicles and possibly even helicopter TV coverage. The Mayor of the host town would have arranged for full road closures and the event would be backed by commercial sponsorship. The Town Square would contain the podium, cheesy euro pop discotheque, dancing girls and a whole array of trade stands. Hordes of Gauloises smoking fans would crowd the café's and bars. The air would be thick with the wonderful aroma of good coffee and freshly baked Croissants.

The reverse is true however in the case of a UK time trial, where you are more likely to see a dozen spectators, standing in the drizzle with a flask of tea and a bored looking dog.

Whilst this is a far cry from the continental cycling scene, it could in fact be a good thing and quite possibly the key to our success. The purpose of this short story is to set the scene of what British TT is about. It might even explain why it has been so successful and still thriving since Thomas Bidlake's vision way back in 1895.

* * *

Beeb bb Beeb Beeb bb Beep goes the alarm clock. It is the alarm clock of rider number 50 whose eyes immediately snap open after having an early night and getting in a full 9 hours of sleep.

'YES, It's race day.' Rider 50 mutters.

Race day is the single most important day of the week for Rider 50 and this day was to be no exception. This is no ordinary race day though. This is the day of an 'A' Race which means that this is one of the most important races of the season to Rider 50 and a race that has been targeted for a victory.

Rider 50 carefully slips a heart rate monitor on and lies still for a few minutes to check the resting heart rate. *Bingo* its 39 beats per minute, the lowest recorded all year. The reason for this is down to the successful training taper which has been executed over the last 2 weeks. It means Rider 50 is at the very peak of physical fitness. Rider 50 has planned the entire season around this day, followed a coach's plan to the rule, eaten the right foods, reached target weight and is ready to race.

Rider 50 is named as such because the event secretary saw fit to prepare his start sheet perfectly and in accordance with the guidance set out in the handbook written by the organising body CTT. There are 72 riders in this race and what this means is that technically there are only two riders on the start sheet who are capable of going faster. Those are the competitors of Rider 60 and Rider 70. Riders 40, 30 & 20 could be dark horses and Rider 10 is a wild card who usually races in another district and unlikely to know the course. Rider 50 won't worry about dark horses or wild cards today though because this is an A Race and Rider 50 is ready to smash it!

So, Rider 50 is a seeded rider. A '0' number and one of the favourites for the win or at least make the podium. The main goal is to win the event which is slightly ambitious, so a fall–back goal is sensibly set to make the podium and win the age category.

But there is a small problem.

* * *

The event secretary now enters the dingy hall. He detects that musty smell present in many of these small village halls. There is also a faint smell of disinfectant close to the toilet. *At least it's clean,* he muses. He manages to source the brass panel of twenty–six light switches and begins a game of light switch lottery. How can there be so many switches for such a small hall? After several minutes of light switching he finally works out which ones light the main room, the kitchen, the ladies, the gents, the outside light, the lobby light, the stage light, the under–stage light, and even the adjoining snooker room light that is situated behind the stage. The lighting is rarely adequate in these old places and our event secretary notices one of the UV strip lights flickering in the rafters. It's one of those old–fashioned types from the 1980's and has a dodgy starter. This is no problem for our experienced event secretary who spots a long broom in the kitchen. One stout whack on the side of the strip light and it springs back into action, a trick he once learned from his father who once looked after the local youth club.

Our event secretary is the 'Average Joe'. Now middle aged, he has enjoyed TT for many years and was once pretty good at it. These days though he prefers to ride for fun and likes to get involved with the club by organising this annual event, which has become one of the most popular 25–mile races on the regions calendar. He also enjoys his role as Secretary on the committee of his cycling club. He is still pretty handy on the bike though and still races from time to time. He is certainly still good enough to teach some of the younger riders a lesson or two on the weekly chain gang.

Our average Joe lives in the average house, drives an average car and lives an average life. He is at the sort of age where his favourite crisps are 'Ready Salted', his favourite TV program is 'The News' and he likes his vegetables slightly over cooked. His favourite clothes are, well anything comfortable, although he has noticed lately that his wife has been buying him clothes which he thinks are way too tight and make him look like a member of the latest boy band.

Opening the event HQ is not quite where our event secretary's story begins though because three hours earlier whilst others were sleeping our man was stealthily tip–toeing around the house trying desperately not to wake his sleeping wife.

* * *

The small problem Rider 50 has is a psychological one because of having never won an open event before. TT can be about mental strength almost as much as it is physical. Rider 50 has been racing time trials for about seven years and with the help of a coach over the last two seasons has done quite well and become a marked rider who many would love to beat. Rider 50 often features on the podium and has had a scattering of second places on the palmares. Rider 50 has also won a few club events but never an 'Open' like this which has been a long–term goal for far too long now.

Rider 50 eats, sleeps and breathes TT and trains specifically for around twelve hours each week and races most weekends throughout the season. Rider 50 strictly follows the guidance and training schedule set by a coach and constantly thinks about kit, pacing strategies, gear ratios, diet and training sessions. No stone is left unturned in the ongoing quest to find those marginal gains to conquer the personal bests which have been previously set.

Rider 50 finishes the small bowl of muesli and drains the rest of the beetroot juice which accompanied breakfast. A fresh pot of coffee is brewed and decanted to a small metal flask which rider 50 will enjoy later at the HQ about an hour before the start. Other than one recent serious doping case, when it comes to doping stories, over dosing on caffeine is about the biggest drugs scandal you are ever likely to hear of in the UK TT scene.

Rider 50 now packs up the car with the mountain of kit required for a TT. In goes the turbo trainer, the bike and several spare wheels. This is an A race, and nothing is being left to chance. The kit bag is slung into the passenger seat, but Rider 50 doesn't bother to check it because that was already done the previous evening and ticking off the habitual checklist. Rider 50 once arrived at HQ still wearing a pair of slippers and so swears by using a checklist to make sure nothing is missed.

The Volkswagen is steered into the country lane and a CD selected for the journey. Rider 50 is not really into music. TT takes up too much time for that but feels it is good to have a song in the head for a race. An up–beat number by 'The Jam' is selected before setting off. Rider 50 noticed a pair of Swallows dancing and swooping through the air collecting insects for their new hatchlings and then swerves the car to avoid the lost looking Pheasant which is now running up the road like a dying Crane Fly whilst displaying an impressive plumage commonly seen on birds from countries with much warmer climates.

The last of the energy drink that was sipped throughout the journey is finished and the car is swung into the car park of the old HQ. Rider 50 is not happy though and spots something in the car park.

Something menacing!

* * *

Whilst our event secretary pads around the house as stealthily as possible desperately trying not to wake his sleeping wife, he enjoys a breakfast of two cup–cakes and a slice of Victoria Sponge which his wife selflessly volunteered to bake the previous evening for the seventy odd hungry racers in his event. With breakfast done he packs the car with all the kit required to run a TT including the all, important race file, result board, race numbers, spare pins, marshal jackets, marshal flags, first aid kit, signing on sheets, route information, police notifications, risk assessments, accident book and a mountain of other paperwork that is required behind the scenes at a TT.

Armed with enough road signs to sink a small battleship packed into the back of the Volvo Estate, he tunes into Radio 4 and sets off into the early hours ready for the important task of pegging out the signs. Putting the signs out is no easy job and takes around two hours on this course even for the most experienced organiser like our event secretary. It can be extremely hazardous too especially on a busy dual carriageway so the best time to do it is in fact during the twilight hours when the only traffic he is likely to be sharing the road with is the occasional HGV rumbling along through the night.

Half way through putting the signs out he spots a few young rabbits in the grass verge running back to their warren as it begins to pour with rain.

'Great,' he curses. He now faces an important decision to make. That decision is whether to continue with the signing or simply abort the event? He decides to continue and finishes the job in the rain and makes his way up to the HQ. He made the right decision as the rain stops completely when he reaches the old hall and opens up.

Before setting up the tables and chairs he washes a few cups and saucers and even starts to tidy up after the 'Weight Watchers' meeting which was held the previous evening. He reads one of the articles out loud to himself.
'This week Mandy lost two pounds and is now close to her target weight', he chuckles, 'these girls should take up cycling.'

The event secretary gets to work with setting up the little hall. All the tables and chairs are stacked neatly against one wall, so he begins to drag a few tables into place into some sort of order. The signing on desk is set up and all the race numbers laid, out so that the riders can easily find them. The spare pins are placed next to them, as too are the signing on sheets complete with spare pens. The chairs are placed into a sociable layout around the hall and he drew back the curtain that was hiding the stage in order to create a little more space. Soon after setting up the HQ he begins to greet the first of his riders and makes the usual small talk with them. He always appreciates their arrival because many of them have travelled a long way and perhaps crossed several counties in order to support his event. He leaves the marshal jackets and red flags by the door so that they can help themselves on arrival

With everything in order, the HQ soon becomes a hive of activity. He now just hopes his marshals don't let him down.

* * *

Beeeb Beeeb Beeeb Beeeb Beeeb Beeeb Beeeb Beeep Beeeb Beeeb Beeeb Beeeb Beeeb Beeeb Beeeb Beeeb Beeeb Beeeb, goes the marshals alarm clock. Beeep Beeeb Beeeeb.......

'Ok, ok shut up for Facks sake,' curses marshal number 5 before rolling over and hitting the snooze button for a third time. The truth is, marshal 5 is not really bothered about today's TT and would much rather be joining the local club run a little later and regrets offering to marshal in the first place. He has already marshalled two events this year and frequently helps out with other club activities. It annoys him that of the eighty odd members in his club, he is among the small handful of members who help out frequently. It is always the same guys who volunteer whilst the majority just slide back into the shadows and make their cheap excuses.

Being completely dedicated to his club, he won't let the event secretary down today, but there is one side of him that really wants to, possibly due to the delayed hangover he will have later on. It is only 6.30am and the first man isn't off until 7.01am. Today he is amongst four others who are marshalling the roundabout at the turn, so the first rider won't be passing his control until about 7:25am at the earliest. No rush then, so he sinks back into the comfort of his bed for a final snooze.

Our Marshal is a bit of a 'Jack the Lad' who loves a laugh and a joke. He is a regular face around the pubs and clubs of his small town and to say he likes a drink would be an understatement. Now in his late twenties he is single after a couple of failed relationships and lives alone with nothing but his beloved cat for company. He bought his first proper road bike and joined the local cycling club only a couple of years ago with the idea of keeping fit, losing weight and getting girls. It was also the first step to changing his previous heavy drinking lifestyle. Since the age of eighteen our marshal fell into a heavy drinking chain smoking lifestyle which would have seen him into an early grave had he continued and he regularly reminds himself of the fact that cycling probably saved his life. He has very much enjoyed the cycling from the moment he started and rarely misses the weekly club run. He just about manages to brush off the stick he gets from his pub mates about wearing lycra, but still enjoys a heavy night out with them some weekends. He has dabbled at TT, but the years of boozing have taken their toll and he is unlikely to feature highly on the local TT circuit unless he drastically changes his ways. He can just about hold his own on the club run and is becoming fitter by the week whilst his weight is steadily decreasing. He always promises himself to one day change his lifestyle completely to become better at the sport he has become to love so much.

A further twenty minutes pass when he is gently awoken by a purring cat licking his chin.

* * *

Beep Beep Beep, went the alarm clock of Rider 49. Rider 49 was already half awake in any case and was dreading the sound of the inevitable alarm clock that was about to signalise his portal into the dark side of cycle racing. This was to be his first ever TT and he was already worried about making a fool of himself in an arena that was completely alien to him.

Rider 49 has only been cycling since the previous July after watching a couple of stages of the Tour De France on television. He was immediately seduced by the sport of cycling and very soon found himself surfing the internet and spending lots of his hard–earned money on an ill–fitting bike and over–priced kit so that he could look just like the professional riders he had watched on TV that summer.

After following the Tour de France and taking delivery of the new bike, Rider 49 started riding all over the place at every opportunity. He read much poor advice and got into his head that the more miles he cycled, the faster he would be able to go.

He joined the local cycling club and was warmly welcomed by all. Some of his new club mates convinced him that TT was a good way to start racing. Unfortunately, they encouraged him to enter a fast 25 in a regional championship event. This is poor advice for a new comer dipping their toe into the world of cycle racing and fast 25 on a dual carriageway is not recommended for any novice and likely to put newcomers off for good.

Nevertheless, our Rider 49 felt he was ready to at least have a go and have a go he did. He borrowed some clip-on aero TT bars which he had never tested before and pumped up the tyres as hard as they could go. If they were pumped up any further, they would have popped off the rims. He stuffed the bike and a few bits of kit into the boot of the Renault whilst appreciating his audience of Chaffinches and Great Tits that were swarming around the bird feeder in his front garden. With the car packed he headed off into unknown territory to start what would become a new chapter and an exciting adventure.

*   *   *

Rider 50 pauses for a moment and takes a deep breath. *Pull yourself together and stop worrying about it*. The menacing sight glimpsed in the car park was that of the car belonging to rider 60! Clearly this means that rider 60 is here and is definitely going to race. It also potentially relegates Rider 50 to second or third place. As malevolent as it sounds Rider 50 now hopes that rider 60 punctures or has some sort of mechanical during his race if the main goal of a win is to be achieved. Whilst Rider 50's hopes for a win might be dashed, there is of course a chance that rider 60 is treating the event as a 'C' race; a non– important race which he is using as training for a more important race later in his calendar. Or perhaps today will be the day that Rider 50 finally turns him over, after all Rider 50 has been snapping at the heels of Rider 60 since the middle of the previous season, but never quite found enough speed to actually beat him. This has been playing at Rider 50's mental strength but perhaps today is the day the tables turn?

Rider 50 enters the little hall that is the HQ and brushes past a couple of club mates blocking the entrance discussing gear ratios and what wheel profiles they are running today. Rider 50 exchanges pleasantries with them before finding a chair in the corner of the hall and pouring the first cup of coffee from the small metal flask. Rider 50 notices Rider 60 on the other side of the room and their eyes momentarily meet while the sweet black liquid is poured.

There are a couple of children playing on the stage, running along and throwing themselves to their knees to see how far they slide on the polished parquet floor. Their angry mother shouting at little Tommy,
'Don't do that you will wear the knees through.'

Two other riders are now standing just opposite, one of them bent over like a downhill skier whilst the other helps him pin his number onto his bottom. A sight, which always amuses Rider 50. It is not quite as amusing though as the sight of the elderly gentleman next to the fire exit who is continuously struggling to change into his skin suit. He has just a small towel wrapped around his waist whilst trying to remain decent. It clearly does not work very well and whilst bending over to pick up his skin suit, the towel keeps slipping to the floor. Arse, bollocks and all are exposed to the amusement of the children playing on the stage. Not a pretty sight.

Rider 50 strolls across to the Event Secretaries desk and signs on very slowly just like all the riders do. They pretend they are looking for their name on the sheet but really, they are secretly scanning and eyeballing the start sheet to see who might be listed as DNS. Rider 60 is already signed in but makes a mental note that Rider 70 is yet to do so. *Could this be the day?* Rider 60 wanders over for a chat with our Rider 50.

'Ok then, how's it going, training much?' Rider 60 asks.
'No mate, the girlfriend had me decorating the bathroom for the last couple weeks, and what with work and

everything, I just don't get much chance these days, I also had that viral thing going around you know, *sniff*, knocked me out for days it did, how bout you?' Replied Rider 50.

'Yeah there's lots of it about, I'm much the same really, just been on me holidays and you know what it's like when you got littluns, there just ain't time to train any more. Anyway, I was out on a bender last night so not expecting much today.'

Rider 50 has no idea what it's like to have children or to have a late night out but nods agreeably.

Of course, what is happening here is a fake conversation anyway because both riders are completely lying through their teeth. Rather bizarrely, they both know this as well because the fast riders rarely give away any hint of their form especially to their key rivals. What they have both in fact been doing is a solid block of training following their coach's instructions to the rule. They have executed near perfect tapers and both are completely up for this race with a view to winning the paltry £30 which is up for grabs to the winner!

Rider 50 goes back to the chair for another coffee and gets distracted by an incoming text message. Rider 50 already knows who it's from and what it will say as it is a bit of a traditional text from the girlfriend before every race. The message reads,
'Good luck speedy pants lol xx'

* * *

Bleep! Sounds the alarm clock of The Timekeeper. There was no need for that alarm to be set of course. For he is the timekeeper, the keeper of time and one of the most important volunteers within the regions TT scene. Timekeepers are and should be regarded as the most respected members of the TT community. After all, whilst many things might influence the result of a TT, a simple scratch of the timekeeper's pencil could be enough to ruin anyone's day!

Our timekeeper is probably the region's most well–respected member of the TT scene and everyone knows and loves him as a gentle giant of a man who is willing to pull out all the stops and do anything to help the local TT community. Of retirement age he is also the coach of many top regional riders, including that of our Rider 50.

He was once a tester himself and raced at a respectable level during his younger years.

The Timekeeper gently glides out of bed and cranes his head towards the clock for a habitual check of the time and curling a knowing smile when he guessed the right time within two or three seconds. Without fuss or undue time delay he gets ready and executes a perfect shave with the freshly sharpened cut throat razor that awaited the owner's artistic hand.

He slicks back his immaculate silver hair, slips into his pristine Savile Row suit and drains the double espresso that he poured while calibrating his stopwatch. He crafts the silk tie into a perfect Windsor knot and splashes on a little cologne before sharpening his pencils and packing the stop–watch and note–book into the lapel pocket.
He makes his way out to the awaiting polished vintage car. The door of the Jaguar smoothly unfolds and the sweet rumble of the V8 engine gently growls over the sound of Mozart which scratches from the mono stereo set into the walnut dash of the classic marque. The timekeeper pulls away from his private drive whilst the dry gravel gently falls from the tyres like dry sand cascading from a dune.

The Timekeeper steers the E–Type towards the main road and winces in sympathy for the unfortunate Long Tailed Tit which he just witnessed being predated by a nearby hunting Hobby in an impressive aerial display. The poor Long Tailed was clearly no match for the speed of this small but impressive bird of prey.

The Timekeeper approaches the village and decides to go straight to the start area in order to synchronise stop watches with the other time keeper and so looks for a suitable place to park up and call the event secretary to explain the plan.

* * *

With the HQ now bustling with activity and more riders arriving, our event secretary begins to feel a bit more at ease. He strolls over to the sign on sheet to count how many have arrived so far and things are looking good. He has taken a couple of calls already from riders who have phoned in to apologise that they can't make the race due to other commitments. He always appreciates the apology when a rider is DNS and so marks DNS (apol) by their name on the sign on sheet and the result board so that the other riders are aware of it too.

Still no sign of the marshals though and this is now worrying him ever so slightly, so he decides to call their mobiles. He needn't have worried though because it seemed four of them were already up at the turn and already had their bib jackets and flags from the last race. No doubt the fifth will arrive soon he tells himself. Arranging marshals is a bit like herding cats, you have no idea what they will do next. He hasn't seen the timekeeper yet either but does not worry about him, he's a time keeper and they are amongst the most reliable living things on the planet. Just as he dismisses the thought his mobile rings and right on cue it's the timekeeper. He has just arrived at the village but just letting our event secretary know he will go straight to the start area in order to synchronise the stop watches with the other timekeeper.

The event secretary goes to the kitchen for a glass of water and opens the serving hatch which separates the main room from the kitchen. He looks out through the hatch to survey the scene.

He can see Rider 50 chatting with Rider 60 and chuckles to himself at the sight of various groups helping each other to pin their numbers to each other. *Always an interesting sight,* he muses. He can over hear the two riders blocking the doorway disputing whether 19mm tubs are faster than 20mm tubs and getting all techy and a bit geeky about rim depth profiles and what they will needlessly waste their money on next. He smiles at the sight of the children running around on the stage and agrees that TT can be a real family event sometimes, although he doubts little Tommy will see much of his Daddy racing today because he will be up on the dual carriageway. He almost chokes on the glass of water he was drinking when he spots one of the older veterans near the fire exit flashing his bits to everyone whilst clumsily trying to get into his skin suit.

'Shit if Social Services ever got hold of this we'd be in for a thorough investigation.' he quipped quietly to himself.
More and more riders pour through the door whilst other riders leave the HQ to get to the start area ready for their respective start times. He takes a look outside in the car park and notices many riders warming up on their turbo trainers. He checks his watch and realises it's soon time for his wife to arrive. His wife loves race day too. She must do because she selflessly volunteered to bake all the cakes last night. She also did all the shopping for the tea, coffee, milk and orange squash that

will accompany the cakes she made. She wasn't so keen though on helping him peg the signs out, so she opted to come out to the HQ and bring along all the refreshments ready for when the first finishers get back to HQ. He smiles to himself and considers himself so lucky to be married to someone who also loves race day.

* * *

Beep Beeb Beeb Beeb, goes the alarm clock of the Race Secretaries wife.
'Shit,' she screams, 'it's race day, I bloody hate race day, and can't believe HE'S put me up to this again! Every bloody year he has to go and organise this stupid race.' She hissed.

This was no ordinary race day though this was his race day. The race, he has meticulously planned and enjoyed for the last couple of months. The wife promised herself after last year that she would never help out again and hoped that he would find someone else to do the teas & coffees. She also tried to hint about just buying some bloody cakes from the supermarket.

'Four freaking hours it took me baking that bloody lot and none of those skinny bastards will appreciate it, and who wants cake at eight o' clock in the morning anyway!' She cursed.

She eventually gets out of bed; she is terrible at getting out of bed on the best of mornings let alone at the weekends. As she gets up and stretches, she notices the jeans she bought him hanging over the door of the wardrobe and grimaces.

'OMG!' She muttered to herself and realises he's only gone out in his old man jeans. 'What must he look like in those old things; they will be laughing at him up at that HQ.'

She eventually gets ready and loads the little Peugeot with all the cakes, tea, coffee, milk, sugar, squash, plastic cups, paper plates and napkins, and heads off to the HQ. She is still cursing her husband and blames him for her lack of sleep. He woke her up at about three in the morning when HE got up, plodding around heavy footed and slamming doors.

'He probably woke the whole neighbourhood up loading that old man's car with all those signs,' she seethed.

With the little car loaded up she sticks the stereo on. It's the Arctic Monkeys for her and she cranks it up to an ear bleeding volume before accelerating off and not even noticing the Lesser Spotted Woodpecker and a Stonechat that she almost murdered in the lane leading up to the old hall.

Upon arrival she weaves through the car–park avoiding the riders warming up on their turbo trainers and parks close enough to the door to carry all the stuff into the kitchen. Fully laden, she squeezes by two riders who are blocking the entrance bragging about the size of their chain–rings and curses them for not even offering to help her. She greets her husband, winces at the sight of his jeans and almost drops the box of cakes when she spots some half naked old bloke getting changed and exposing his backside.

'WTF!' Were her only words.

*   *   *

There we have it again, 'Unspoilt by money,' demonstrated by the typical HQ for a TT event. A typical HQ for such event might be a scout hut, primary school, community room, village hall, occasionally a lay–by in the middle of nowhere or if you are very lucky a pub, will be the location of the Headquarters. The HQ often lacks facilities such as changing rooms, showers, restaurants and even electricity in some cases. Do we really need all that though? Of course, it would be nice to have extra facilities, but many racers arrive at the HQ in their kit in any case and usually in a hurry to get home after the race where they can shower in the comfort of their own homes.

The typical HQ such as a village hall has its charm in many ways and often a talking point amongst the riders. I am told by my Cornish neighbours that the HQ for one of their events used to be a public toilet on the edge of the small village of Fraddon just outside of Truro. Another HQ I visit frequently is that of a pre-school room. Each time I arrive I feel like Gulliver because everything is in miniature. It is a sight to behold, seeing grown men and women sitting around discussing gear ratios etc., whilst sitting in a chair designed for a four-year old.

For me these old HQ's have great character and form an endearing part of this curious sport's scene. I also should confess to developing a slightly weird interest in the topic!

* * *

The Timekeeper swings the E–Type into the start lay-by and the second he engages the handbrake the other time keeper rolls to a halt just behind him in an Aston Martin DB6 as they arrive in perfect synchronism. They have arranged to meet here so that they can synchronise their stop watches. Our timekeeper is manning the start today so with the stop watches synchronised, the second timekeeper heads off in the DB6 for the short journey to the finish area, where he will greet his assistant and set up the chequered board.

The Timekeeper sets up the start area by giving the area a little sweep with the shortened broom that he keeps in the boot and places a line precisely on the start using a length of industrial duct tape. He then places two cones either side of the line signifying the start house where the riders will start to queue in anticipation of their race.

The pusher off arrives in the start area and greets the timekeeper. For the next 72 minutes this will be their place of work. Rider 1 is called with 1 minute to go before the start. At 30 seconds the pusher off holds the rider and machine upright whilst Rider 1 clips into his pedals. The time keeper counts down 5 4 3 2 1 Go, and the race begins. Rider 2 is next up. Then it is the turn of rider 3 who chucks his jacket at the timekeeper without even saying a word and just expecting him to carry it back to HQ for him. The Timekeeper gives the rider a hard stare before turning a blind eye to the rudeness. This is unfortunately, a common occurrence with riders who have warmed up out on the road with warm clothing such as a cycle jacket or gloves. Most riders ask politely, and the timekeeper will always happily oblige and place all the clothing in a box which he keeps in the boot of the Jag. There are however, one or two who are less polite and just throw it at the volunteers as though they are about to make a depart at the Tour De France!

One by one the riders are set off at one–minute intervals as more riders arrive in the lay–by to await their respective turns.

* * *

'Shit, Shit, Shit,' curses the marshal as he carefully pushes his cat Dennis off the pillow. He has overslept and must have pressed stop instead of the snooze button on the alarm clock. He is now so late and in grave danger of letting the event secretary down. He only has about half an hour to get out of the flat, race out to the HQ, pick up his reflective marshal bib & flag and then drive out to his control point at the turn.

'I can still do this.' He murmurs and very quickly feeds Dennis. He then downs the cold cup of tea and troughs the last slice of cold pizza which were both left on the bedside table; A usual habit of his after a night out on the beer with the lads. His mobile phone is next to the pizza box and starts to vibrate indicating a phone call. He checks the screen and doesn't bother to answer, it's the event secretary who is probably wondering where he is, so he ignores the call and slips the neat little device into the pocket of his jeans.

With no time for a shower, he splashes on a bit of aftershave and rinses his mouth with mouthwash, just in case the 'Old Bill' are patrolling his area. From past experience and a little bit of 'previous', he is well aware that the 'Busies' will be out in full Breathalyzer mode, especially so early on a Sunday morning! Christ, the truth is he had such a skin–full last night that there is no way he would be below the legal driving limit and would probably blow a positive should he get stopped! Whilst he doesn't really want another brush with the law, he is also dedicated to his cycling club and would never let them down, so he stupidly carries on tearing around the upstairs flat to get ready. He hears a baby wailing and a dog barking followed by what sounds like a full on domestic between the young couple in the flat below and feels bad as the realisation sets in that he probably caused this with his running around in a mad last–minute panic.

He quickly disregards the thought and races out to his waiting car which is parked outside. The sound of the heated argument and barking dog soon recedes as he approaches the car. He tears open the door of the shagged–out Fiat and prays that it starts. He's only had the car a few months and it has been dogged with electrical problems and let him down on too many occasions. He breathes a sigh of relief when it guns into action on the second attempt.

Just before he pulls away he spots a lone Magpie on the window sill of the downstairs flat and curses his luck; one for sorrow and all that! But the 'Townie' in our marshal doesn't believe in all that folklore bollocks

anyway and again disregards the thought. There are also two Urban Gulls squabbling over the take–way pizza box which they have expertly dragged out of the bin bags. The bin bags which the students from the opposite flat have once again managed to put out on the wrong day!
'Lazy bastard students,' he mumbles, 'I suppose muggins here will be clearing that lot up later.'

With the Fiat now running he checks the mirrors for patrolling 'Filth' and races off to the HQ. It is only a short drive to the village, but he constantly keeps a check on those mirrors and races up the country lane without noticing any of the hedgerow nesting birds who are avoiding the speeding car up the lane leading to the old village hall. He dumps the Italian rust bucket right outside the door because there is no time to park it properly and he leaves the engine running, just in case he can't get it started again. He rushes into the HQ barging past the two riders who are chatting and blocking the doorway, discussing the benefits of titanium saddle rails and runs into the hall tripping over the box of red flags and marshal jackets that the event secretary helpfully left by the door. He peers through the serving hatch to offer a quick apology to the organiser for his lateness and receives a look of relief from him as he

reaches over to help himself to a flapjack and a couple of cup–cakes. He overhears Rider 50 and Rider 60 chatting about how crap they are feeling today.
'Yeah, right, lying bastards.' He sniggered.

The marshal pulled a face at the kids on the stage to tease little Tommy and then spots the virtually naked old bloke baring his arse to everyone in the HQ.
'Flippin el mate put it away and use the bogs will ya there's kids in ere look.' He shouted whilst giving a cheeky wink to little Tommy's Mum.

With no more time to entertain everyone in the HQ he grabs his marshalling bib and flag, jumps back into his old banger and floors it down the lane taking a short cut he knows, threading the car down a nearby farm track which later joins the main road which gets him back onto the dual carriageway. He's still got a few minutes to spare before the first rider is expected but still thrashes the little Fiat to its limit all the way out to the turn, passing several of the riders who are now on their race and settling into their rhythms. About a mile from the turn he overtakes Rider 1 and breathes another sigh of relief because it means he's made it. The marshal expertly abandons the car onto the grass verge and puts on the reflective bib while running across the roundabout to join the other marshals. He reckons he's still got a minute to spare before rider 1 comes through so stops for a quick chat with one of them.

'Alright mate, told you I wouldn't let ya down dint I, ow long you been waitin ere then?' He quipped smugly.

'Ere, youm lookin ruff this morning bud. Shit, you stink as well, you been on the piss again? You wanna hope you don't get stopped mate you smell like a bleedin brewery. Anyway, you reckon our Rider 50 will do the business today then?' He asked our Marshal.

'Do me a favour mate that one's well past it.'

* * *

Rider 50 finishes a thorough warm up in the car–park on the turbo trainer and consumes a quick energy gel as the start time fast approaches. The turbo trainer and kit bag are packed away into the boot and the rear wheel switched out in favour of a full disc wheel for this day. Rider 50 then habitually checks the tyre pressures before setting off on the bike to head to the start area.

Now, for our Rider 50, there is only one thing worse than the sight of Rider 60, and that is the sight of Rider 70, who is later seen warming up on a turbo trainer in a lay-by at the village.

'Dammit'. Rider 50 cursed.

This means that the favourite is going to race after all and probably planning to sign on after warming up.

Rider 70 is the best rider in the district and wins pretty much anything he enters. He is certainly good enough to challenge some of the best riders in the country at national standard. Had he been 20 years younger he would have probably joined the professional ranks and possibly even world stage competition. Throughout his life, Rider 70 is one athlete who appears to be excellent at everything he does. At school, Rider 70 was head boy; he would have been the teacher's pet, a noble breed, the leader of the pack, the captain of the team and the boy that all the girls fancied. Rider 70 can do no wrong and everyone wants to be like Rider 70.

* * *

Rider 50 tries to push the thought to one side to focus on something that the coach is always banging on about. He is always reminding Rider 50 to forget about the other guys. 'What they do is out of your control. Control only the things you can change.' The coach would reiterate.

Rider 50 looks up at the St Georges flag which is hanging motionless from the spire of the village church which is a very pleasing sight. This of course means little or no wind at the moment but noted on the forecast that the wind is due to get up through the morning. Testers call this a rising wind, which is great for the early starters but not so great for the guys starting near the end like riders 50, 60 & 70. Rider 50 also checked the air pressure for the day and at below 1000 millibars indicated lower than average air pressure. More pleasing news as low pressure usually equates to a faster time.

Rider 50 soon arrives at the start area and spots rider 49 in the lay-by who will be today's minute–man. Rider 50 notices an ill–fitting race pin on the back of the novice looking rider number 49 and so calls him over. Rider 50 helpfully pins him up properly and wishes him the best of luck before doing a couple neck stretches and cleaning the visor of the aero helmet.

* * *

The work of the start timekeeper and the pusher off is almost complete. There are 72 riders in the race and the next rider to go off will be the very nervous looking Rider 49 who is about to start his first ever TT. The experienced timekeeper senses this immediately so he calms the rider with his soothing tones of encouragement. He further reassures his new friend that everything is fine and that there is plenty of time to get clipped in. The experienced pusher off can also sense new blood, because new or novice riders are often difficult to hold up at the start. Rider 49 leans one way then the next whilst awkwardly clipping in to the pedals and physically shaking with fear. A rider's first TT can be a daunting experience, but it is a process that is quickly learned. Rider 49 although leaning a little too far to one side hears the time keeper count down 5 4 3 2 1 Go and appreciates the little encouraging shove he is given by the pusher off. He is then blasted by the horn of a less respectful lorry driver causing the poor newcomer to wobble violently before nervously joining the dual carriageway.

'Shame,' said the timekeeper, 'we probably won't see him back. He really should have chosen a sporting course for his first race and not a fast 25 like this, but never mind.'

Rider 50 is next up and with years of experience, expertly rolls into the start house with 15 seconds to go and manages to track–stand whilst the pusher off expertly holds the saddle with a single hand. Rider 50 didn't even need to speak or unclip from the pedals such as the experience of both rider and pusher off. Rider 50's machine stays perfectly still and they both make the process look seamless. Whilst Rider 50 zero's the power meter, the time keeper who is also rider 50's coach gives a quick word of encouragement to his rider before counting down 5 4 3 2 1 Go and rider 50 calmly and respectfully thanks the two volunteers whilst simultaneously springing out of the saddle to make a perfect 'Depart'.

The remaining riders are set off at their respective start times including those of the two big favourites, Riders 60 & 70. With everyone out of the start house our Timekeeper and Pusher Off, instinctively pick in all the signage in the lay-by to assist the Event Secretary later. They also load up all the sweaty jackets, warm up wear and the odd dirty drinks bottles that were thrown at them at the start by some of the less respectful riders. The Timekeeper packs it all into the box and returns it to HQ for collection. The cones are packed, and the duct tape peeled off the road. Both volunteers then make their way back to HQ to be rewarded with some tea and cakes for their efforts.

* * *

Rider 50 quickly settles into a rhythm and is bowling along the dual carriageway with effortless looking motion. For the first few minutes the power meter is a nudge below target average power which is right where it should be for the first few minutes whilst the heart rate steadily climbs to race pace. Only 5 or so minutes after departing rider 50 catches the minute man and blows right past him like he was standing still. Poor Rider 49 must have wondered where on earth Rider 50 came from but can only be impressed by the display of speed being demonstrated as all he can do is watch in awe as the roaring sound of rider 50's disc wheel very quickly disappears into the distance ahead.

Rider 48 is caught, then Rider 47, just as the first of several road-side photographers are passed making for a potentially good shot. Our Rider 50 is eating up the road and the pain is beginning to kick in. Rider 50 invites the pain in and keeps a careful eye on the power meter which is now averaging exactly where it should be in order to nick a PB and quite possibly the victory. With gritted teeth and a slight grunt Rider 50 is now completely in 'The Zone' and focussed on the job in hand. With the cranks ticking over like a metronome, the upper body rock solid and the aero helmet perfectly synchronised with the riders back, it really is an awesome display of near TT perfection.

The turn is approaching now where there are a couple more photographers and 5 marshals waiting. With this being a 'home' race, the marshals start shouting encouragement to rider 50.

'DIG IN DEEP. YOU CAN DO IT.' One shouts.
'COME ON MATE THIS IS YOUR DAY.' Cries another.

With the half way point passed rider 50 is in a good place and doesn't feel too fatigued just yet so ramps the power up just slightly as the heart rate is settled and if anything is slightly lower than expected. This is always a bit of a gamble and tempting by some riders, but it can run the risk of losing power in the closing stages of the race.

Still in the zone and completely focussed on the job in hand, there are just 2 miles left to race. Rider 50 passes another rider and spots that St Georges flag on the spire of a village church in the distance which is still just hanging limp and motionless indicating that the wind didn't get up as forecasted; a pleasing sight.

'Yes,' rider 50 mutters, 'this is a fast day!'

The chequered board comes into view with about 250 metres to go and Rider 50 digs in deep for a final big effort and getting it all out, lighting all the matches all the way up to the finish where the time keeper awaits in anticipation. Rider 50 shouts out the bib number to the timekeeper whilst simultaneously checking the stopwatch. It's going to be oh so close to a PB. There are just seconds in it but only the official result will count which will be displayed at the HQ a little later. There is nothing more that can be done now other than wait a while to find out what times the riders 60 & 70 managed to post.

With the chain engaged in the small ring, Rider 50 spins a light gear for the journey back to HQ and will complete a regularised cool down on the turbo trainer back at the HQ car park.

* * *

As each rider passes the chequered board in their various states of fatigue and dizziness, they have the agonising task of riding back to the HQ. The experienced riders will appreciate this as it can be used as part of their strategic cool down where they will spend much time spinning light gears whilst travelling the four miles back. The less experienced will race back as quickly as possible as though the cakes are about to run out.

Regardless of experience, the pulse rate of every rider will now be receding whilst our event secretary's pulse rate starts to increase dramatically. Such increase is due to the inevitable presentation and speech that he is soon due to deliver as part of his responsibility as event secretary. The presentation marks the end of the race for many and usually consists of a short speech by the event secretary, who will thank all the volunteers, followed by the prize giving to the worthy winners. It also, provides opportunity for the event secretary to remind all the riders to sign out before they leave. This is something that the CTT can be very strict about and can lead to a DQ if ignored. Some event secretaries enjoy delivering the presentation and use it as a chance to tell one or two terrible jokes and pretend they are a stand–up comic for a few minutes. Many other organisers, including our man, get very nervous and usually end up missing someone while thanking everyone for their support.

While the hall slowly fills with riders returning from their races, the noise levels rise, and the hall becomes ever so slightly cramped. The two children who were playing on the stage are now sat quietly with their Mum and getting into a sticky mess with a flap jack, the two riders that were blocking the entrance are now mingling with others in the hall, talking about how tough the wind was and making excuses for their piss poor performances. The half-naked man has decided to keep his skin suit on and not even attempt to get changed in the hall after his embarrassing encounter before the race. Rider 49 is making new friends and being warmly welcomed by a couple of experienced riders who are keen to provide the newcomer with advice. With new friends made he feels much better and is already planning his next race and will be back. The race secretary's wife is run off her feet serving the teas and coffees and silently cursing every rider behind a forced smile. The marshals are returning one by one and dumping some of the road signs in the foyer for the race secretary to sort out later. The time keeper and pusher off arrive with more signage and all the jackets and warm clothing that the riders threw at them in the start area. Riders 70, 60 and our rider 50 are outside in the car park on their turbo trainers executing perfect cool downs before consuming recovery products and putting on their compression garments to aid their recovery.

Everyone else is inside the hall drinking tea and eating cake while the event secretary studies the timekeepers result sheet and carefully starts to fill in the result board. The result board is a large white board which he fills out with a marker pen. The riders swarm around him like paparazzi around a film star, all jostling for position trying their best to get a glimpse of their resultant time while they are written up one by one. There are the inevitable whoops and some gasps of disbelief within the crowded hall as the times of the seeded riders are posted for all to see particularly with the times of riders 50, 60 & 70.

The noise levels rise to a crescendo when the last of the results are posted and the crowd of riders desperately push and shove whilst trying to take a photo of the result board with their mobile phones. This very almost marks the end of the morning for many of the race goers. The only task left is for our event secretary to deliver the presentation.

He swiftly hands the prize money envelopes to each of the respective category winners after delivering his short nervous speech where he thanked all the marshals, photographers, the two timekeepers, the pusher off and of course to his wife for selflessly volunteering to run the kitchen and bake all the cakes.

With the event complete and the result delivered the noise levels drop considerably and the hall is empty within minutes. Soon, the only people remaining in the old hall are the event secretary and his wife who are left to tidy up.

His wife is busy in the kitchen washing the dishes and cleaning up the remainder of the refreshments. The event secretary loads up both, his and his wife's cars with the signage that the marshals helpfully picked in and returned for him. He collects up all the odd items of clothing that inevitably get left behind by the more forgetful riders. He loads the rest of the race files into the Volvo and drags all the tables and chairs back to where he found them. He gives the floor a bit of a sweep, checks the toilets are clean and finally takes the rubbish out to the collection point. Even the marshals have cleared off now but to be fair to them they didn't need to hang around any longer and they all did a splendid job on the day. The Event Secretary really does appreciate all the help he has received from the usual club mates. The marshals were even thoughtful enough this time to pick in the signage on their journey back to HQ, thus saving the secretary a further 25–mile drive.

With both cars loaded the event secretary fumbles once again with the unfamiliar keys to lock the slightly rotted door. He takes a final glance back at the hall and gives the door a final shove to ensure it is secure.

'Never again.' He mumbles.

He doesn't really mean this of course because deep down he knows that he won't be able to resist and will come back next year making the event even bigger. Bigger prizes perhaps? Possibly a sponsor or a proper podium? Rest assured he will return for more next year and for many more years to follow.

* * *

Crumbling old HQ's, the rallying around of organisers, the selfless work of volunteers, the work of the organising body CTT and much, much more are all the things that make the sport happen and make it happen well. It simply IS 'Unspoilt by Money' and quite probably the key to this wonderful sports success. It has worked very much the same way for several decades and I really hope that it remains that way.

On October 5th 1895 when Frederick Thomas Bidlake decided to organise that first ever TT, I sometimes wonder if he really knew what would come of it. After all cycle racing was banned because it scared the horses and interest was declining rapidly. He must have had a real burning desire to continue to race and to encourage others to do so whilst pretending to go about their usual business. In hindsight this seems a rather extreme thing to do to avoid Police attention. Whatever his reason, it was a genius idea pure and simple and it still lives on today in the format that we know and love.

During the weekends of the Spring & Summer months, all over the country whilst most people are still sleeping there are dozens of these events being held by the hundreds of cycling clubs in the UK. Think of the many event secretaries, the timekeepers, the photographers, the marshals, the tea girls and boys, and of course the riders themselves all working hard to make this happen?

Somewhere near you at about 5am on a Sunday morning, there will be an event secretary pegging out the colossal amount of signage for a race. By the time most people are awake and go out for the day, those signs will have all been picked in as if nothing happened at all. All these volunteers should in my mind be applauded and commended for their hard work. The events are backed up by the work of the CTT which also relies heavily on volunteers. As far as I am aware the organising body only has two full–time paid staff and a further two part–time. The rest of the work is picked up by the volunteers who fill the seats on the Board of Directors and District Committees.

The format of the sport has not changed much since 1922 when the first organising body was formed. Ok the machines have changed dramatically, and we know a lot more about the sport science stuff, but the concept remains the same. Man, machine, and a stopwatch. What can simpler than that? Since the concept hasn't changed since well before my time, I can't see it changing very much long after I'm gone either. One day when I am gone, and my niece and nephew come to clear out my loft, I like to think, they might come across a load of old rotting bikes and other cycling junk. They might even find the few corroding medals and trophies and realise their Uncle was once quite good at something; and not just the bloke who turned up at Christmas each year.

For me the attraction of TT is in fact the 'Unspoilt by money' part of it. I know I keep returning to this line but for me it really is true. It is the old halls, the selfless volunteers, and the rubbish prizes. Ok so some clubs occasionally try to glam it up a bit by attracting the sponsorship of a bike shop. They might offer a few spot prizes like a tyre, a track pump, a cheap bike computer or a water bottle to supplement the small cash prizes on offer. The prizes are not really rubbish when you consider the cost of entry to an average open TT is only around the price of a couple pints of beer. The cycling club then needs to pay to hire a HQ and pay a small levy to the organising body. They may even need to cover some additional expenses for refreshments and of course the club needs to make a small profit so that their club can survive and to be able to maintain the equipment required to run future events. Whatever is left is given out in prizes for the winning categories.

As well as being unspoilt by money, I have found this to be a friendly sport too. No matter what a rider's ability, they will always be warmly welcomed by all, they will mix with the top riders and from my experience everyone gets on well. It's almost like one large family, a union of people, particularly if you race frequently and within your home district. You will begin to recognise faces and those faces will seem to be at every event you go to. You will make many friends along the way on your TT journey. You will recognise who is at a similar ability to yourself and start pitching yourself against them. They may even become your close rivals but never your enemies. Most of us try to pitch ourselves against a slightly better rider. It gives us something to aim at and goals to set. Before long you may notice others doing the same to you as you progress.

Each year I never want the racing season to finish and feel sad when September finally ends. For many it means that you won't see all those wonderful people who make the sport happen again for many months. It also means that winter is just around the corner. A time when we all lock ourselves away into the turbo trainer room! It is a strange thing when you arrive at the HQ for the first race of the season. It's like being reunited again with your summer family. There's always a lot of hand shaking going on and people young and old wishing, 'Happy New Year,' to each other.... In March

So, it's the HQ's, it's the people, the TT community; the family that make it all work like a well-oiled machine. There is that old saying. 'If it isn't broke, don't fix it', and this is so true in terms of TT. Of course, improvements are probably possible, but they are very minor, and everyone has differing opinions in any case. I am a firm believer that the current formula is correct and that it does not need changing too much. It's true that the majority of 'Testers' seem to be veterans and there does seem to be a slight lack of younger riders coming through but in fairness this is only partially true as we have recently noticed a small increase in younger members, particularly after the success of the 2012 & 2016 Olympic Games. It is also true that many of the old HQ's lack facilities such as changing rooms, showers, heating or air conditioning or in some cases even electricity. Improved HQ facilities may be possible but such venues like hotels, conference rooms and fancy leisure centres become too expensive for the average club to afford and likely to wipe out any profit made and result in increased entry cost. This could in turn result in a fewer number of entries, so we need to tread very carefully when considering improvement.

In UK TT there are no overhead banners at the finish or open–air podiums, live entertainment or dancing girls. Ok some clubs may try and give it a professional touch by erecting a gazebo and perhaps some of those advertisement banners that resemble a boat sail in an attempt to tidy the place up. I even took part in one National 25 event which had a start ramp built, similar as that used at the Tour de France. It might have only been knocked up with a few sheets of MDF in someone's garage, but I applaud that volunteer who no doubt gave up a lot of their time and effort to provide it for their club.

Unspoilt by money. Remember this and remember the people, the TT community who make this happen and get out and support them, join them, sing it from the roof tops if need be, but most of all just enjoy it. It doesn't need lots of money to make people happy. TT is the purest form of cycle sport and always will be. It has survived since 1895 without too much fuss and long may it live on.

Arrivée

Rider 50 didn't achieve her goal of a win today. That award went to Rider 70. She didn't even feature on the podium either, because Rider 60 took second place and remember that wild card from another district? Well he took the remaining podium spot. Rider 50 clearly didn't see that one coming.

She did take fourth place and achieve the fall–back goal of winning her category so it's not all doom and gloom, although she is slightly disappointed with missing her PB by just a single second on what was looking like a fast day. To Rider 50 it was a complete disaster and she feels quite depressed about the result. Considering her recent form, the good conditions and near perfect preparation she was expecting to do better and record a PB at the very least. TT can be infuriating at times but wonderful when things do go right.

After packing all the kit back into the VW, she quietly slips away from the HQ to head home. With the stereo switched off she drives home in silence with her mind racing and searching every corner of it to find what went wrong. The truth is, nothing went wrong, she was probably shooting a little higher than her current level of ability, but nonetheless she continues to think about it and is already planning and thinking about the next race and how to beat Rider 60 once and for all.

The Tour de France theme tune trills from her mobile phone breaking the silence and indicating a new text message. It's her girlfriend again.

'Hi babe can you drop into the supermarket to get a few bits bread milk juice cat food oh and chocolate SYL xx.' Read the message.

She quickly swings the car around to retrace the three miles back to the nearest supermarket, ever so slightly cursing the late request. She is still wearing her skin suit and with her body completely drained after the race, she now has to plod around a supermarket looking like a strangely dressed alien.

She very swiftly scoots around the aisles filling the small basket, ticking off the short shopping list and avoiding eye contact with the other customers who are wondering why there is a battered looking woman in a leotard limping around the shop. As she makes her way to the '10 or less' checkout she spots the latest 'Cycling Weekly' in the magazine rack. There is a feature headlined 'Italian Legends' on the front cover which caught her eye, so she picks up a copy. She can now feel the eyes of the check–out boy boring into her as she fumbles with the envelope containing the winnings she got for winning her category to pay for the goods. She would later realise that he was probably staring at the white salt line she is now sporting on her upper lip as well as the blood shot eyes and the bulging vein on her forehead which she often experiences for several hours after a hard race.

With the shopping packed into the boot, squeezed between a disc wheel and a turbo trainer she heads off once more soon arriving back to the piece, and tranquillity of her rural home. She steps into the living room dumping the shopping onto the small coffee table and slumps into the arm chair without even bothering to unload the all the kit, which she would do later.

'Howdit go Speedy Pants,' Came the cry from the kitchen.

'Oh, not too good,' she replied, 'fourth place and first woman.'

'Well cheer up then that good isn't it?' She enquired.

'Yeah, I guess. Just thought I'd do better though and that Rider 60 skinned me again.' She grumbled, 'Oh I got those bits you wanted.'

The girlfriend entered the living room passing her a chilled recovery smoothie she had waiting for her return and snatched the chocolate bar she got her in exchange.

'Never mind babe you'll get him next time,' she reassured, 'Just put your feet up, I'll have lunch ready in no time.'

Feeling a bit more refreshed after the smoothie and encouragement from her girlfriend she starts to feel happier and rummages around the shopping bag for the cycling weekly she just bought from the supermarket. She drops the magazine onto the table and it immediately falls open to a page with a large picture of the Italian legend, Fausto Coppi. She looks at the picture for a couple of seconds and almost felt the sparkle in Fausto's eye freeze her to the spot. She shudders for a moment and feels that prickling sensation as the hairs on the back of her neck rise and looks again, this time smiling and reading Coppi's famous quote that is written next to the picture.

'You Beauty.' She said to herself very quietly. 'That's what it's all about.'

She smiled once more and glanced back at the picture again to read the quote. The line was short yet effective, it was pure yet controversial. It was simply beautiful and read: –

Ride your Bike.
Ride your Bike.
Ride your Bike.

Fin

Lantern Rouge – A Beginner's Guide

Whilst the purpose of this book is not intended as a training guide, I wanted to include a section specifically for riders who might want to dip their toe into the racing world and explain why TT would be a good place to start. I am not a coach, so I am not going to go all technical about it and start setting training zones or discussing Functional Threshold Power and aerodynamics. The following passages are intended for beginners and are driven purely from my own experiences as a coached rider and how I went from absolute beginner to achieving my goal of winning an open event.

Why TT?
Ok so we have already identified that we Brits are very good at TT, but it does sometimes make me wonder why it is not as popular as some other areas of cycling. Cyclo–

Sportives it seems are currently the most popular discipline in cycling and attracts UK riders in their hundreds. More popular sportives such as the Dartmoor Classic and the Fred Whitton Challenge sell out very quickly and allow many thousands of riders to enter, yet TT and possibly to a lesser degree, road racing appear to suffer with much fewer entries.

To be honest this is not always the case in some regions of the UK as a few events particularly on the fast courses become over-subscribed. Many events allow up to 120 riders but in regions such as the South West most races typically attract only 30–80 entries. Whilst this is still viable, there is certainly room for improvement. Such improvement would be welcomed by all who are involved with TT including myself and the cycling team I represent.

The act of cycling is the most efficient transformation of human energy into land based forward motion. Time-trialling is the purest form of exploiting that movement into competitive cycle sport where only the strongest rider wins.

Whilst Time–trialling and Road racing are both fantastic sports, they are both very different from each other. This book is not about road racing, but a simple comparison might help establish the objectives of each. Personally, I prefer TT but that is because it suits my strengths more than bunch racing does. I know many riders who compete in both forms of racing although most spend more time doing one or the other. Many other riders prefer to not try either and simply stick with Cyclo–Sportives, which is still good because they can be great fun very sociable. However, they are not competitive races like Road Racing & TT are.

TT is often misunderstood; possibly because it is not called a 'race.' Some say that TT is not a race but only a test against yourself. I could not disagree more because it most certainly is a race. Everyone has their opinion of course, but not everyone fully understands the concept of a TT.

The objective of a Road Race (RR) is to cross the finishing line before as many riders as possible however there are various strategies of how this can be done. Collaborations may be made with other riders, teamwork from your team or club mates may come into play, getting into the right break or making an attack at the right time could also affect the outcome. There are endless ways to tackle a RR and each one is different, making it a fantastic sport to watch unfold.

It is often about race 'craft' and judging other rider's abilities. It can be very tactical and rewarding yet frustrating as the strongest rider is not always the winner. The fundamental difference between RR & TT is that in a RR you ride in a mass start with many other riders. In a TT you ride alone.

So, in a RR you can draft other riders saving up to 40% energy staying close to the rider in front. If a gap forms, the forces of drag against you and your bike become greater and you are forced to begin to work harder, using up valuable energy stores in order to close that gap. If you are a novice rider and that gap opens up even MORE, you may not ever get back on to the bunch and your race is basically over. This can be a particular problem for the novice rider as they could potentially pay a lot of money to enter a race and be out the back of the bunch, heading for an early shower after just a few minutes of racing. I have witnessed this, and it does not particularly sell amateur RR well to me.

The objective of a TT is to also cross the finishing line faster than as many riders as possible. None of the other riders though are your friend and there will be no collaborations made, not even with your club mates who may be in the same race. This is because all the riders are set off at one–minute intervals, so it is therefore a pure test of speed where you ride alone.

So, in a TT you cannot draft other riders and the force of drag against you is the same for everyone. What this does mean of course, is that if you are a novice rider, no matter how your race goes and providing you finish, you will be given a time and placing at the end. If it is your first TT, that time will be your PB. Your legs will hurt during the event and you might even for a moment wonder why on earth you are voluntarily inflicting such pain. But once you return to the HQ you will already be thinking, and you will already be planning on how to break that PB next time.

Who Should TT?
Virtually anyone who enjoys riding a bicycle can TT. The only rule in the UK is that you are aged 12 years or over. At the other end of the scale, there are riders still going

under the hour in a 25–mile TT who are well into their 70's.

TT is enjoyed by many disabled riders too, as can be seen at the Paralympic and Invictus Games. I know a man with one leg who enjoys TT. His bike has been especially adapted at the bottom bracket so that his prostatic leg remains static whilst he pedals with the other.

TT is also enjoyed by organ transplant patients. I have another friend who is a transplant patient who featured at the World Transplant Games including the TT event. Many events also allow tandems to enter which is great as this allows the blind or partially sighted to enjoy TT as well.

So virtually everyone can TT possibly because it is very much an endurance sport and not high impact like running, football or rugby. It is therefore a sport which can be enjoyed at or near to your true potential for many decades. Whilst I know of some riders in their 70's still racing with excellent results, I am sure the same cannot be said for many other sports.

Most UK events present prizes for various categories. Such categories include Junior's and Juvenile's. Men/Women Senior's and Men/Women Veteran's. Often, there will be a Veteran on 'Standard' category, which allows an age handicap which factors their age into their performance.

So, do you want to be the next Rider 50, Bradley Wiggins or Beryl Burton? Do you enjoy riding your bike and wish to add a competitive edge? Or do you simply want to improve your fitness and gain the ability to ride your bike FAST?

If the answer is YES to one or more of the above and you don't mind inflicting a little pain to yourself, join a cycling club who is registered with the organising body CTT and read on.

Getting Started

Getting started in TT is very easy. The best way you can do this is to join your local cycling club. If you plan to ride a lot of TT's, it is important to choose a club that has an active TT scene and is registered with the organising body CTT. Most cycling clubs have a website or sometimes a flyer at the local bike shop so it's not too difficult to select a suitable club.

Virtually all clubs hold a weekly club run at the weekend so just go along and ride with them. If you enjoy it and decide to join the club you will be very warmly welcomed.

There will a race or event secretary at the club who will be happy to help you with how to set about racing and will even help you with your race entry if required.

Unlike RR, you don't need a licence to race TT. For open events you simply need to be a member of a club that is registered with the organising body CTT.

Ok so you have joined a club, you have a road worthy bike and are already pouring over the CTT handbook or schedule of TT's passed to you by the race secretary. Right? Good. The next step and this for me is possibly the most important decision you make in your TT adventure. That step is choosing a **suitable** event for your first race. Don't start like our Rider 49 did in the preceding story.

I will be brutally honest here, but not all courses are suitable for beginners and I know of many people who tried TT once, hated it and never returned, simply because they chose a fast 10 on a busy dual carriageway. This would be enough to put anyone off TT before they even start. Not all races are on busy roads though. Many are held on quieter 'B' roads and are often referred to as 'Sporting' courses. If it is your first race, these types are perfect as there is usually very little traffic and they are often held in scenic countryside.

It is also a good idea to use one of your own club events for your first TT. This is not essential of course, but you might be more comfortable in your own surroundings. You will know people if it's organised by your own club. You might even know the time keeper and all the marshals. The marshals will probably even give a few words of encouragement as you pass them in your race. I would not recommend driving half way across the country to a fast course where you don't know anyone or even where the start, finish and HQ are. Not for you first event anyway.

So, we have found a suitable first event. The next step is to know the course. Hopefully it will be a local 'sporting' course which might even be on roads you already know well. Needless to say, you need to know exactly where the start and finish are, and preferably ride the course a couple times in the weeks building up to the event. If you don't know the course and it's within reasonable distance from where your club meets, suggest a club run out to reconnoitre the course the weekend before. Your new club mates will probably be happy to do this. They may even be entered in the same race.

Ok, you have got the bike, joined a club, selected a suitable course which you have ridden before and know well. You are now almost ready to a start your first ever TT.

A few days before your race you obviously need to ensure your bike is in good working order. Take it to your local bike shop for a service if there is anything troubling you like sticky gear changes or worn tyres.

Lay all your kit out the day before to make sure you have not forgotten anything. It is amazing how often I see even the most experienced arrive at HQ having forgotten their helmet or shoes.

If the race is early in the morning, ensure you eat a carbohydrate rich meal the night before. A nicely balanced pasta dish is good. I find rice dishes work well too such as Paella or Risotto. The meal the night before is far more important than what you eat on the morning. On the day you should eat something about 2 hours before your start. Perhaps a small bowl of cereal such as muesli or porridge. Try to stay hydrated throughout the day and sip an energy drink in the morning while travelling to the event.

With breakfast done, it is now time to pack the car. Obviously remember your bike, spare wheels if required, tools and a pump. Next you need to make sure your bag has everything inside. Helmet, shoes, socks, HR monitor and skin–suit etc. If you plan to warm up on a turbo trainer, don't leave it behind. The turbo is not essential but is recommended for a better warm up. Make sure you have clothing ready to wear after the event. Finally have a little spare cash. Some events ask for donations towards the refreshment funds.

Most of this stuff is common sense but it really is a good idea to keep a checklist and make sure everything is packed. I once went to a race and felt sure everything was packed. Everything was packed but I got 10 miles into my drive only to discover I was still wearing my slippers!

Once you arrive at HQ, you need to sign on. This is just a simple procedure of signing the start register to confirm you are racing. You will then take your race number to pin to the lower back area of your jersey or skin suit. Please note that you must also sign out at the end of the race when you return your race number. This is extremely important as failure to do so might lead to a

DQ and we don't want that to happen with your inaugural race. Next, you need to get warmed up which is absolutely vital.

Warming up properly can become quite scientific to some and I have seen all manner of warm up styles from simply rolling around the start area through to complex warm-ups executed on turbo trainers whilst studying numbers on lap–top computers. The permutations are endless but a good place to start would be to give yourself at least half an hour warm up which should include a gradual build up to tempo intensity and 2x2 minutes at your race pace. You need to get that engine smoking hot and have a light sweat going when you get to your start. Try to be at the start area a few minutes before your start time on your first race. As you become more experienced you will be able to shorten this to just a few seconds, particularly if you have synchronised your clock with the time keeper like some of the experienced riders do. You will be called at about 30 seconds before the off. There will be a pusher off to hold you and your bike up for you while you clip into your pedals. The time keeper will countdown. Five, Four, Three, Two, One, and your off. Good luck and congratulations, you are about to set a PB.

Goals

Ok you have now completed your first ever TT and you have recorded a Personal Best (PB). As this is now the start of your new found go faster obsession, we now need to focus on how we are going to smash that PB and think about setting a new one. A good place to start, before we do any fancy training sessions or buying some go faster kit, is to sit down with pen and paper and set some goals.

It is important to set goals as it gives you something to aim at. It can be an art form in it–self but hopefully the following guidance will help you along the way with setting your TT goals.

If you have ever been coached in cycling or any other sport, or if you have ever been on some sort of corporate or business training course, you have probably heard the following Acronym SMART. This stands for: –

S – Specific
M – Measurable
A – Achievable
R – Realistic
T – Time–framed

This can be a useful acronym, but when setting goals in sport, we need to expand a little wider and split those goals up into 'Racing Goals' and 'Training Goals'. A step further still and we can expand again into short term and long–term goals. Let's take a closer look at SMART.

Specific. These goals have a greater chance of being accomplished than a general goal so always try to be specific. A general goal would say, 'I want to ride my bike fast'. But a specific goal would say, 'I will train three times a week to ride a fast TT'.

Measurable. A goal must be measurable which is in fact quite easy in TT. Racing results are measurable, so a measured goal might say, 'I want to break 1hr for a 25–mile TT'. If you have a turbo trainer, it is quite possible to measure your progression by using a 20–minute speed test. So, another example might say, 'I want to average 25mph in my 20–minute speed test'.

Achievable & Realistic. I always think that these two are pretty much the same thing in terms of sport. Goals must be achievable or otherwise you will always fail. Failure unfortunately breeds failure, so ensure the goal is achievable and realistic. It's no use having a goal to say, win the Olympic Games TT, if for example you are 40 years old and just started cycling. That is an over simplification, but you get the picture. Breaking the hour for a 25-mile TT is a common goal and more likely to be achievable. Make some interim goals too such as 1:02 or 1:01 for a 25. You are more likely to succeed with your goals by breaking them down into sub goals. Remember success breeds success.

Time-framed. Always try where possible to include a time frame for the goal, otherwise there is no sense of urgency. So instead of saying, 'I want to lose weight'. Say, 'I want to lose 3kg before the start of next season'. This makes the weight loss goal specific, realistic and time-framed.

So, a good example of a specific, measurable, achievable, realistic and time-framed racing goal might be: –

'To break 1 hour in a 25-mile TT by the end of next September'.

This is a great example of a long-term racing goal, but you then need to set some training goals and some short term interim goals in order to achieve that main racing goal. A short-term training goal could be simply a weekly mileage target. A target that pushes you slightly but is just about realistic for the time-frame you set yourself to train each week. That is a great short-term training goal. We are now building a picture of how we are going to achieve that original goal of breaking the hour. You may wish to set some interim measurable goals too such as a target Functional Threshold Power if you are using a power meter.

So, we now have a long term and some short-term goals. We also have racing and training goals all in accordance with the SMART rule.

Before we finish discussing goals I guess I should mention that it is very important not to set your goals in stone. They should be constantly reviewed and if necessary amended. You may be achieving goals more quickly than anticipated, or you might be missing the timeframes for other goals. It is a fine balancing act but can be very rewarding when you achieve your goals as a result so revisit your written goals frequently and refresh them as and when required.

It is also important to be flexible with your goals. Be creative not just in goal setting but training as well. Try different approaches and training methods and find what gives the best improvement. Remember the following saying: –

'If you always do what you always did, you will always get what you always got'.

This is so true in TT and if you stick to the same goals and events from year to year, you will never truly progress. Remember, be creative, be flexible, be organised and frequently review and amend your goals in order to unleash that true potential.

True Potential
What do I mean by true potential? Surely the only way we can reach our true potential would be to start our TT career at the age of 12 and dedicate our entire life to the sport, right? Correct.

Furthermore, this would require bunking off school and riding our bikes for around 20,000 miles a year, for several years spending around 30 hours in the saddle each week. We may then by our early 20's be lucky enough to become full time professional racing cyclists and have access to the best equipment and coaching possible.

Add to this several sessions of wind tunnel testing to optimise aerodynamics and we should then be very close to that true TT potential.

As lovely as that all sounds, such dedication to the sport is rare and not realistically possible for the average amateur club cyclist whose goal might be to win some club silverware or even take victory in the occasional open event.

Clearly true potential is just not possible for most of us due to a common obstacle many of us stumble upon. That obstacle is called 'life' and it has the annoying habit of getting in the way of our professional racing careers.

So, if 'life' wins and we just can't become full time pros, what can we achieve? Well it is quite possible to get very close to your true potential with much less time and dedication than you might think. Three time Tour de France champion and crack time–triallist Greg Lemond, once said that 10 hours a week is all the training required to ride at a very high standard in short distance TT's.

If you plan to ride short distance TT's of up to 50 miles this is so true and even proven by many top UK Testers including some National Champions. It would not be the case however if your ambitions were to compete at multi stage races such as the Tour of Britain or even the Tour de France, but let's face it, most of us won't get that opportunity. So, you really don't need to spend as much time as you might think to ride a fast TT or to win a road race.

Some riders are able to dedicate more time than this, perhaps even fifteen hours per week, but there is divided opinion upon whether this would actually help the average club rider excel in short distance TT. In fact, it could even be detrimental to some riders TT performance as their aerobic capacity may not be underpinned by the colossal volume of endurance training that is necessary for such training stress. Sometimes less can be more. Don't be tempted to always train as hard as you can or otherwise you will never actually get the opportunity to train as hard as you really can. Two really, high-quality training sessions per week will be much more beneficial than say four compromised sessions where you are simply tired before you start.

Even if you are very aerobically fit and able to handle fifteen hours of TT training per week, those extra five hours may only get you a handful of seconds in a 25–mile TT. But the implications of your lifestyle, family, friends and job are likely to be significant. Such training load is also very demanding on the body and would require much focus on recovery and nutrition.

During my first few years of racing time–trials, I made many mistakes. One such mistake was in fact just this, doing too much and not training smartly.

I started my first full season at the age of 36 after many years of simply riding for fitness and completing a few long–distance 'Audax' events. I also enjoyed the occasional tour including riding from John O'Groats to Land End. As my interest grew in TT I read as much literature as possible on the subject which included some poor advice. I held the popular belief that it was all about miles and the more miles you did the faster you will get. I read much advice about spending the majority of your time riding at a low intensity over long periods, increasing aerobic capacity in a progressive manner. This would have been great if I wanted to only ride Cyclo–Sportives, but in hindsight it did little for TT.

In seasons 2 & 3 I used my work commute as the bedrock of my training. I would get up at the crack of dawn and ride twenty or thirty miles before work. Then ride another thirty on the way home clocking up to three hundred miles or more each week, all based on the poor advice that this would somehow improve my TT performance.

I still occasionally kick myself for the mistake but possibly shouldn't be too harsh. This time–consuming method to a certain degree did help as I was still breaking PB's. Furthermore, I enjoyed it, even when I was battling against harsh conditions day in day out. It helped because it made me fitter and I became very efficient on the bike. The last time I checked though, TT was not an efficiency contest, but a SPEED competition. What I was in fact doing was training myself to ride slowly. In fact, I became so great at riding slowly that an eighty–mile club run at 17mph was like a walk in the park. The problem was that my target TT speed was more like 28mph and those long rides did very little to help this other than provide a sound base.

TT is about specifics. What I should have been doing was riding way less miles and spending more time at or above that target speed of 28mph. Contrary to popular belief, in order to be able to ride your bike fast, you are going to have to at some point, well you know, ride your bike fast. Remember the more you do something the better at it you will become. If you want to be a sprinter, do some sprints. If you want to climb mountains, climb mountains. If you want to ride at 28mph for an hour, guess what? Clearly, I fell into a trap by following some bad advice which at the time seemed logical.

It wasn't the least bit logical.

So, anyone who can spend around 10 hours per week following some sort of structured training program with their coach and riding at the correct intensity is likely to excel in TT. Of course, you don't have to train for 10 hours per week; many riders get by with much less with excellent results.

The great thing about TT is that there are lots of levels of achievement you can aim for. Your current level of ability is likely to feature somewhere on the list below: –

- Racing your first TT
- Not coming last in your category
- Smashing PB's
- Hitting a target FTP
- Going under a certain time for a given distance
- Beating your close rivals and friends
- Making the top ten at an Open event
- Reaching 05 or even 00 status
- Winning your category
- Making the top three at an open event
- Winning some of your club's silver
- Winning a club event or series
- Winning an Open event
- Breaking a club record
- Breaking a course record
- Success at your regional BAR competition
- Aiming for National success
- Aiming for World stage competition

The above list can be useful and used as part of the goal setting section discussed earlier. Draw a line under where you are now and where you want to be in say, 12 months? Revisit your written goals and amend as necessary as you progress? The journey to succeeding with your goals is often more fun than the destination.

Ultimately, if you are going to get close to your true potential, it is going to take up a lot of your time and have impact on your life outside cycling. It is about finding balance with your work, family and friends. It is about weaving high quality training sessions between your more important work and family commitments. You need to set goals and timeframes in which to train and get the support from family. It can be about giving time back and earning the 'Brownie Points' to go about your new-found obsession. Be organised, be creative, be flexible but most of all remember Fausto's words.

Training

So, we have set some goals and touched on what our potential might be. Training is going to play a large part of your life if you are to achieve those goals, so it is a good idea to set much time aside for such. I have already stated that this book is not aimed to be a training guide, program or bible but does cover a few ideas on training and what equipment should be required in order to achieve training some training and racing goals.

When I started TT I usually finished in terms of placing around the middle to bottom of the field so was pretty average to say the least. In a typical 25–mile TT my time would be around 15–20 minutes slower than that of the winner and I marvelled at the times those top guys were recording. It just didn't seem humanly possible for a person to hold that kind of speed for such long periods at a time. This inspired me to take TT to the next level and soon I was posting similar times and reached the level of achieving my goal of winning an open event and much of my club's silverware. How did I do it? Correct training was the key.

I feel duty bound to once again mention that I am not a coach, but a coached rider who understands how to train properly for TT. I am not your coach and I do not know anything about you, your goals or your current level of ability. Therefore, it would be impossible for me to set a training program for you as an individual other than explain general training issues such as warming up, cooling down and stretching.

My advice in this arena would be to initially obtain a training book specific to TT and simply try some of the sessions described. Don't do as I did and start riding hundreds of miles a week at a slow pace, thinking that this will make you fast. Remember, training should be specific to what you want to achieve. If you want to ride at a certain speed over a set distance, such as one hour for a 25– mile TT, you need to spend much of your training time at that intensity. If you want to be a sprinter, do some sprints. If you want to climb mountains, climb mountains. I f you want to be able to ride at 25mph for an hour, you know what you need to do. There is no silver bullet in training and everyone is different so one athlete's program may not be suitable for another. As well as using a generic training program, there is much information on the internet and various forums specific to TT. These can be useful but tread carefully as to what advice you heed because there is a lot of false information available so be as specific as you can be.

The best way to progress in my mind is to invest in a coach who can specialise in TT training. This might sound exotic and perhaps expensive. However, the benefit of having a coach will far outweigh the benefit of a similar investment in kit or the purchase of a better bike.

I hope that the reader will be able to draw their own conclusions and either invest in a coach or by developing their own training program through trial and error. Good luck.

Dynamic Stretching

Before we commence any vigorous exercise like a training session or racing a TT, we should spend around 15 minutes performing loads of stretching exercises in order to prime our bodies into what we are going to ask it to do right? Wrong again!

This was once common wisdom amongst athletes and I still occasionally see it today. You may have seen such practice at the HQ where some riders are limbering up by touching toes, pulling their heel towards their buttocks, stretching their necks and so forth. They all hold the popular belief that this is going to somehow help their TT performance, but in fact the reverse is true, and it is likely that they are destroying their true potential.

Such stretching exercises were once encouraged by gym instructors and sports experts. The theory being that stretching primes our muscles ready for action and helps to prevent muscle injury. Modern research however turns this conventional wisdom on its head and has identified that this type of stretching is in fact detrimental to performance and even more importantly, has discovered that such stretching is more likely to cause injury rather than prevent it.

When we stretch a muscle beyond its normal limit, it immediately contracts and begins to try to correct itself. Basically, we are asking a cold muscle to start working before we want it to do anything, which is not good. Stretching exercises such as touching toes, putting a leg against a fence and pulling your knee to your chest are known as 'Static Stretches'. They do have their place but should be performed after exercise and not before. They are very important and form part of your recovery. We will discuss Static Stretching a little later.

So why am I talking about Stretching anyway? **'Dynamic Stretching'** is the answer. Dynamic stretching is a type of stretch which involves replicating what we are about to do. So, it is in fact a stretch carried out on the bike by pedalling at a very low intensity.

If you have ever watched a professional tennis match like those at Wimbledon you have probably noticed that before the game, the players warm up on court by lightly knocking the ball back and forth to each other for several minutes. This is their dynamic stretch and forms a vital part of their warm up routine. Ever watched a football match? The players do very similar by gently passing the ball to each other and lightly jogging around the pitch. They might dribble with the ball then violently throw themselves on the floor and roll around like they are a victim of sniper fire, before getting up waving arms around and swearing at the referee. The dynamic stretch should replicate what we are about to do.

So, a dynamic stretch for TT training or racing would be to pedal very lightly for several minutes in the TT position. I usually allow about five minutes for this on the turbo trainer spinning a very small gear and keeping the HR very low. You don't have to do this on a turbo trainer of course, you could perform it on the road but just be careful not to start too hard and avoid any hills for the first few minutes as the effort should be very light.

The Dynamic Stretch should be seen as a sort of warm up to 'The Warm up'.

The Warm Up
I feel that this is the appropriate juncture to introduce another favourite acronym of mine. That acronym is the 6 P's. If you have ever been on some sort of corporate or management training course, you may already be familiar with this. The 6 P's stand for: –

Proper Preparation Prevents Piss Poor Performance.

I simply cannot stress enough just how important it is to be properly warmed up before we race or even tackle a hard training session. A race may not be won by a proper warm up, but it can certainly be lost. The purpose of this passage is to identify and explain why it is so important and why it must not be compromised. We will end the discussion with what sort of warm up should be done for what type of event and set an example that is specific for a TT.

The warm up generally consists of a gradual increase in physical activity in order to bring the body to a condition at which it can safely respond to nerve signals for quick and efficient action. In summary it prepares the athlete both mentally and physically for action.

The direct physical affects of a good warm up are as follows: –

–Release of adrenaline
–Increased heart rate
–Enabling oxygen in the blood to travel with greater speed and higher volume
–Increased production of sunovial fluid within joints
–Efficiency of joints
–Dilation of capillaries

- Increased temperature in the muscle
- Decreased viscosity of blood
- Facilitation of enzyme activity
- Encouragement of dissociation of oxygen from haemoglobin
- Decreased viscosity within the muscle
- Greater extensibility and elasticity of the musle
- Increased force and contraction
- Increase of muscle metabolism
- Supply of energy through breakdown of glygogen
- Removal of lactic acid

It is important to note that the warm up should differ with what type of event you are preparing for and there is a general rule of thumb that the shorter the race, the longer the warm up should be. For example, if you are about to go touring, no warm up is necessary. For a 4-hour training ride or long distance cyclo–sportive, simply unloading your bike and pumping up your tyres would probably be enough. For a road race, 15–30 minutes spinning on rollers is probably sufficient to get the juices flowing, particularly if there is a neutral zone for the first mile or so. For a 10–mile TT a progressive warm up on a turbo trainer for up to one hour would not be uncommon.

So, we have identified the principles of a warm and explained the physiology. It is now time to present an example session, however before that I would like to introduce yet another acronym. That acronym is KISS and stands for: –

Keep It Simple Stupid.
Whilst the warm up for a race is extremely important, I also believe that it is equally important to keep it simple so that it is remembered well and forms part of our usual habitual routine on race day. I only race time–trials of up to 50 miles so my warm up routine is the same for every race in order to keep things simple and takes 30 minutes on the turbo trainer regardless of the event distance. This goes slightly against the general rule that the shorter the event, the greater the warm up should be. However, I don't want the stress of trying to remember different routines for different distances as there is enough to be thinking about on race day as it is.

As well as seeing guys simply roll around the start area for their warm up, I often see others warming up at the HQ with all manner of complicated routines. One guy I know keeps a large sheet of paper in the window of his car which he follows meticulously, and I have also seen people warming up whilst studying numbers on lap top computers displaying numbers from their power meters. For me this just adds unwanted complication and I prefer to use one routine which I have rehearsed and know well. I don't need anything in front of me dictating what I do next. I always carry out this warm up on the turbo trainer with my training wheel and tyre installed. Here is my warm up routine:–

Race Day Warm Up	**30 minutes**
5 min	Dynamic Stretch in Zone 1 (R)
5 min	Zone 2 (Easy spinning)
2min	Zone 3 (Brisk slight panting)
2min	Zone 1 (Very light spinning)
2min	Zone 3 (Brisk slight panting)
2 min	Zone 1 (Very light spinning)
2 min	Zone 3 (Brisk slight panting)
1min	Zone 4 (Hard effort)
1min	Zone 5 (Race pace)
8 min	Zone 3 (Brisk slight

	panting)
Total 30min	Change rear wheel and head to the start.

The above routine was tailored for me by a professional coach and I found it suited me after trying several other strategies. It is easy to remember and is relatively simple. I also use this routine the day before a race in order to practice it. As I say it works for me, but it may not be the one for you. Try it and if it works, great, if not keep juggling ideas until you find one that works and then make it a habit.

Dynamic stretching and the Warm up can be carried out on the road, however this can be difficult due to junctions, hills and headwinds. It also runs the risk of getting a puncture before you get to the start area. So, the best way to warm up for a race is by way of the turbo trainer.

The Turbo Trainer.
The turbo trainer is likely to be the most important piece of your training armoury and the first thing you should rescue if your house is on fire. It is sometimes described as an instrument of torture that clamps your bike to a

resistance unit by the back wheel allowing you to train on your TT bike at home without the disruption of traffic out on the road.

For TT training, I cannot begin to explain just how important it is to own a good quality turbo trainer. Virtually every hour of my training of necessity is carried out on the turbo trainer. The reason for this is that much of my training for TT is carried out at around my FTP which is quite a high intensity and requires considerable concentration. So, it is simply not possible or even safe to do this for long periods whilst out on the roads and mixing with the traffic and other road users. Much of my training is also done on the TT bike whilst in the aero position in order to train my body to hold the aero position for long periods at a time. It would not be safe or advisable to try this out on the road other than during a race where there are marshals and signage warning other road users of the event.

There is a whole array of turbo trainers on the market today ranging from the very cheap through to the super expensive and from past experience I have found this is an area that you really do get what you pay for. There are generally three types of resistance units found on turbo trainers; magnetic, fluid or wind. Magnetic units have a reputation for being quieter than some. This is not always the case though and largely depends on the quality. Fluid units have a reputation for being smooth with a road like feel and a longer coast down. Wind trainers have a very long coast down and simulate the road best, however, even the most expensive items are extremely noisy. I am not going to mention any brands, but I would recommend a quality fluid trainer with a very heavy flywheel and long coast down.

I have owned three turbo trainers now, the first of which was a cheap magnetic trainer which after just one year of light use, caught fire and fell to pieces. I then invested in a slightly better magnetic trainer and the bearings failed prematurely. My current trainer is a heavy–duty fluid type with a progressive resistance unit, heavy flywheel and large diameter roller. It has served me well and after 6 years of heavy abuse and literally thousands of miles, it still runs like new.

The disadvantage of training on a turbo trainer is that you tend to get quite hot and you will appear to sweat much more than you do out on the road. You don't actually sweat more; it just feels that way because of the lack of wind that tends to dry your sweat quicker when out on the open road. The best way to combat this is by setting up a large fan in front of the trainer. This won't simulate the air out on the road perfectly, but it certainly helps to keep cooler whilst tapping out the miles.

If turbo trainers are not for you, the alternative might be a set of training Rollers.

Rollers

I have always viewed rollers with suspicion, or possibly just fear. However, they can provide a valuable addition to the training armoury of any cyclist regardless of experience in their use.

One of the benefits of rollers compared to using a turbo trainer is that they may help improve your balance and bike handling skills. If you struggle on the road during a race with holding a straight line, then you might benefit from the balance and core stability training that rollers provide.

Another advantage is that of the high cadence workouts that can be performed on rollers which is said to help develop a smooth and efficient pedal stroke. I however view this claim with caution and don't necessarily agree with trying to change cadence for TT. I am a firm believer that optimum cadence comes naturally. This is likely to benefit road racers more than it does testers as cadence changes and quick accelerations are required for sprinting or chasing down a break. Furthermore, it is quite possible to perform high cadence work on a turbo trainer by using smaller gears in any case.

It could be argued that rollers present a more interesting workout than riding a turbo trainer because you have something to concentrate on, but this is only partially true. If you have a planned session on a turbo trainer you will have something to concentrate on because you will be following a plan. It is not advisable to jump on a turbo or rollers and simply pedal without a plan as boredom will become more likely.

Another advantage of rollers is with the ease of setting up. This is a clear bonus because you can simply ride straight away without the need to clamp the bike to the resistance unit. This might be useful for warming up at an event as it removes the need for setting up and changing the rear wheel. It is important to use a training wheel on a turbo trainer as they tend to wear out tyres quite quickly, so it is advisable to use a turbo specific tyre on the training wheel. It is not advisable to use an expensive tub on a turbo trainer, but this is less of an issue with rollers. The ease of setting up does not affect me whilst training at home because the bike is already set up and only ever removed from the turbo on race day.

There are some disadvantages of using rollers too, the first being that you need to invest some time in learning how to ride them. This can be an art form in itself and can be tricky to begin with, but after some time you will build confidence and be able to spend much time tapping out a rhythm without the fear of falling off.

The most fundamental disadvantage with rollers is that you simply cannot generate the forces that you can on the turbo trainer. For me this is a major issue and the reason I no longer train with rollers as I found it difficult to safely maintain the required intensity for long periods at a time. Some types of rollers do come with resistance fans that help with this, but it still does not really simulate the true effort required whilst out on the road during a TT.

You have probably realised by now that I am a firm believer that training should be specific to what you intend to do. Time–trialling involves curling up into a near foetal ball and riding your bike so it makes sense that any training done for TT should be done in the TT position.

Training in the TT position

As I have previously stated, when I started TT I was doing pretty much everything wrong and this was just another area where things were going wrong too. During my first few seasons I did almost all training out on the road and on a standard road bike. Most of the time would be spent at quite a low intensity and riding on the brake hoods. Then at the weekend I would head out to a race with the TT bike. At the time it made sense because that's what it seemed most people did. Looking back, it made no sense whatsoever!

Fast forward a couple years and I took the help of my coach and one of the first things he wanted to know about me was what bike I trained on and whether I owned a turbo trainer. He explained the reasoning and the penny dropped immediately. From that point on he encouraged me to train on the same bike that I raced on. Remember, be specific. Today, other than riding club runs, pretty much every hour of my training of necessity is done on the TT bike on the turbo trainer and in the TT position. It makes perfect sense when you think about it as TT is a very specific sport. I am sure that Formula One racing driver's, would not execute most of their training in a family hatchback car. So, if you are planning on finding your true potential in TT, why on earth gamble by training on a different bike than you race on?

During some research on social media, I asked many of the testers in my region the same question and I was quite staggered to hear some of the answers. One or two pure testers did train only on their TT bikes, some combined their training and trained on both TT & RR bikes, but the majority only ever trained on road bikes out on the road and the majority of those never competed in road races at all. Their reason being, that they don't like turbo trainers. Some even said they didn't want to get their TT bike dirty whilst out training. I can also tell you having studied many result sheets that there was a definite pattern forming.

You might not be too surprised by this, but I can report that the individuals who trained on their TT bikes and in the TT position were the riders with the better TT results!

Now do I have your attention?

So why is training in the TT position better? The most obvious reason is specifics and it just makes perfect logical sense. Another reason is adaptation and your body will become more efficient at riding in the extreme position. No matter how much training you do in the TT position, it will never be truly comfortable however it will become LESS uncomfortable over time. When I started training on the TT bike in the TT position on the turbo, I immediately noticed that my HR would rise dramatically when I moved down into the TT position whilst maintaining the same power. I experimented with this over time by riding on the horns at a given power and speed and recording HR. I would then move into the TT position and I would notice this HR spike. This indicated that I was riding more efficiently whilst upright and that I was NOT as well adapted to the more aerodynamic TT position. This was probably due to all that training spent on the road bike over many years. So, I persevered under coach guidance and continued training in both positions and after several months I noticed that the HR would rise slightly less whilst in the TT position. This was because I was slowly adapting to the new position. Eventually and after some considerable time of training only in the TT position the reverse was true. In fact, I started to notice that HR actually DECREASED whilst in the TT position, indicating that I had become MORE efficient in the TT position than I was whilst riding upright! All this extra speed was for free by simply training in the TT position. Try this over time and I am sure you will find the same. Clearly if you become more efficient at riding in the TT position, you will be able to generate even more power in that position giving you a double bonus. Not only will you be generating more power and speed, but you will also reap the benefit from the aerodynamics and so be even FASTER.

If you decide to heed this sound advice and start training in the TT position, don't be too surprised if at first you find it very difficult. It takes time to adapt to a new position and to become efficient. One way to do this is to try position intervals. So, for example if you are riding a 20–minute interval, ride the first minute on the horns and the next in the TT position. Try alternating this for the whole 20 minutes with a minute on and a minute off. Then try 2 minutes on and 1 minute off, then 3 minutes on etc. Keep practicing until eventually you are able to stay in the TT position for the entire length of your intervals whilst keeping an eye on the Heart rate monitor to judge efficiency.

Heart Rate Monitor

The heart rate monitor (HRM) is a personal monitoring device that allows one to measure heart rate in beats per minute in real time or record for later study. If you are looking to get the best out of your training, a HRM is going to be an essential tool.

As with turbo trainers, there is a wide range of HRM types available from the very cheap through to the super expensive, however it is worth noting that for cycling you are likely to also require a cycling computer as well as a HRM. In order to avoid having too many accessories attached to the handlebars it is a good idea to go for a combined cycle computer that has a built in HRM. There are several brands available but most well-known brands are likely to suffice.

If you heed the sound advice of executing much of your training on a turbo trainer, it is important that your combined computer/HRM has a rear wheel sensor as well so that it can be used on the turbo trainer. Some brands measure speed from a sensor that is deigned to record from the front wheel. This is obviously going to be pretty useless for recording rides on the turbo as the front wheel remains static. Some computers operate from a GPS signal which can be beneficial. If you choose this type, ensure that you also purchase the rear wheel sensor so that it may be used on the turbo trainer.

Most good HRM computers can record current speed, average speed, current HR, average HR, distance covered and total time elapsed. It is also worth choosing one that has a lap function so that information during intervals may be recorded too. If your budget allows a cadence function might be useful so that you can find your optimum cadence. A good computer/HRM with a cadence function can cost as little as the price of two or three quality tyres or about the price of a night out with your mates.

Listening to your body and monitoring heart rate is one thing but understanding what it is telling you is an altogether different story and a good place to start would be by setting up some heart rate training zones. The problem with heart rate training zones is that there are just so many systems available leaving it open to much guess work. I have counted around 42 systems in total which of course all make bold claims that their method is best. In truth though no matter which system you choose, there will always be a blurred line between zones. The most accurate way is likely to be by way of a Vo2 max and blood lactate test. There are so many variables however that even this method may be inaccurate. There will never be a true line where you, for example change from zone 2 to zone 3. I am therefore not going to provide any further advice relating to training zones but can tell you that no matter what training session is undertaken, it should be followed by a proper cool down.

The Cool down

We discussed earlier at great length the topic of warming up and focused on just how important it is. Well some might argue that cooling down and finding a good cool down routine is equally as important as the warm up. A race probably won't be won or lost by a good cool down but cooling down properly is likely to aid recovery in order to increase the quality of your proceeding training session or race. Increased quality training sessions are just one small thing that we can add to our aggregation of marginal gains, so correct cooling down might contribute greatly to your next race performance.

You might have noticed whilst watching the Tour de France recently that some of the riders now have cool down routines which they perform straight after the race each day. It was British Rider Chris Froome of team Sky who appeared to pioneer this at the Tour and very few other riders took heed at first. 3 victories later and other riders started to take note. In fact, most of the professional riders now adopt this approach and can be seen near the finish cooling down on their turbo trainers post race.

The cool down generally consists of a gradual decrease in physical activity in order to bring the body temperature and heart rate back to the state it was in prior to the physical activity. Aside from bringing temperature and heart rate down, the cool down also helps to dispose of the waste products and toxins that were generated during the training session or race. The most well-known waste product is lactic acid. If this is allowed to build up in the body, it can cause stiffness and cramp to the muscles the following day. Cooling down can also reduce the risk of dizziness at the end of a race which can be caused by suddenly stopping physical activity.

I should add that all my training sessions end with a cool down of around 5–10 minutes spinning very light gears and until the HR lowers to below 100bpm. This however is usually insufficient following a race where cooling down takes longer. Depending on the distance from the race finish and the HQ, I usually put the bike back onto the turbo trainer and spin a light gear at a high cadence for around 15 minutes or until the HR has subsided to below 100bpm.

With the training session and cool down complete its time to do some stretching.

Static stretching
A little earlier we discussed Dynamic Stretching which is a stretch done on the bike. Static stretching is not stretching done on the bike, so it can be done pretty much anywhere. You could even do much of it whilst standing in a car park or in the HQ after a race. What is more important, is that stretching should be carried out after racing and not before, and it forms a vital part of the recovery process.

I only carry out 6 stretches and the whole routine is completed in just a few minutes as soon as I get off the bike as follows: –

1. Quadriceps stretch. (pulling foot back towards buttock)
2. Hamstrings stretch (touching toes or similar)
3. Lower back stretch (forward bending stretch)
4. Adductors, groin and hamstring stretch (lunge position)
5. Gluteus Maximus Stretch (pull knee towards chest)
6. Upper back and shoulder stretch (arms stretched up)

Off the Bike Training

I am going to keep this as short as possible. This is because, and you have probably already noticed that it is a strong opinion of mine that any training of necessity for TT should be carried out on the bike and in the TT position on the turbo trainer. Other than one simple core exercise, I am a firm believer that any training done off the bike is a futile.

I often hear other riders tell me how weight training, swimming or running has helped their cycling. It may well have helped their cycling and probably helped it more than sitting in a pub would have done. However, the question they never ask themselves is whether it helped their cycling as much as MORE cycling would have done?

I know that there is much divided opinion on this subject and many readers will completely disagree with me, but the following passages should help to explain my reasons for being so matter of fact on the subject and why I truly believe that most 'off the bike training' is a waste of your limited and precious training time.

If you are anything like me and have a limited time to train and race TT, why gamble with that precious time doing anything else other than 'On the Bike Training'?

Take heed of Faustos' words:
'Ride your Bike Ride your Bike Ride your Bike.'

Swimming
Swimming is a fantastic hobby and provides an excellent cardiovascular workout. It also works almost every

muscle in the body and is very gentle on the joints. If I am ever forced to give up TT I may choose to take this up for general, all over body conditioning and keeping fit.

As swimming is very much an aerobic sport it does in fact correlate quite well with general cycling. Clearly if you compete at multi-sport events such as triathlon, swimming is going to play a major part in your training and should be done regularly.

If you are a pure cyclist and looking to find your true potential in TT, I am afraid my advice to you is to stay well away from swimming other than an occasional visit to the local baths or a dip in the sea whilst on holiday.

Ever watched Olympic swimming on the telly? Take a look at the athletes just before they dive in and race. The first thing you notice about their physique is their massive shoulders.

Like TT, swimming is a very specific sport and they didn't get those shoulders by weight lifting, they didn't get them by running and they certainly didn't get them by cycling. They got them by endless hours of specific swimming and those strong shoulders are vital for pulling their bodies through the water.

For time–trialling, large shoulders are the last thing you need as aerodynamics play a fundamental part of TT. Large shoulders equal greater frontal area which means greater drag and more power required for the same speed. This will in turn result in a slower time.
Like I say swimming is a great cardiovascular sport and a very enjoyable activity. It is unlikely that you will develop large shoulders form the occasional dip, so by all means go swimming but don't use it as a substitute for 'On the Bike Training'. After all I am unaware of any top cyclist who said. 'Swim Swim Swim'.

Running
Many of my cycling friends are runners too who enjoy competing at half marathons and other similar distance challenge runs. If this is your thing, by all means do lots of running to supplement your cycling. If, however you are a pure cyclist looking to achieve your full potential in TT, I reiterate that running is unlikely to help you TT any faster and might even be detrimental to your cycling performance. Again, it is about limited training time so

why gamble with that time by running when more cycling is obviously more specific to your goal.

As an endurance sport, running once again correlates quite well with cycling as it is a cardiovascular sport and great for body conditioning. Some say that running uses different muscles than cycling and is therefore a waste of time. This however is only partly true because in fact running exercises the same leg muscles that cycling does. The difference is how you use them and the firing sequence in which the muscle fibres are recruited.

If you enjoy running and wish to compete at the odd half marathon or charity run, by all means go running, however if you wish to find your true potential at TT I would advise against substituting your valuable cycling time to go running. After all I am unaware of any top cyclist who said. 'Run Run Run'.

Weight training

Ever watched professional cycling on telly, such as that of the Tour de France? You have probably found yourself the envy of these professional guy's legs. After all, I am sure this is the only reason that my girlfriend shows such keen interest.

Don't be fooled however into thinking that they got those legs by going to the gym and doing loads of leg bearing exercises or doing lots of running or swimming. They got those muscles by 'On the Bike Training', hour upon hour, of training and racing <u>on the bike</u>.

I often hear friends telling me how they plan to do lots of gym work over the winter as they too think that this will somehow make them a better cyclist. Once again, I am sure it will help to a degree and more than sitting in the pub would do. Will it help as much as more cycling would have done? I very much doubt it.

If you have time to spare and enjoy going to the gym, by all means go but I would advise against using the gym as a substitute for on the bike training. After all I am unaware of any top cyclist who said. 'Lift weight Lift Weight Lift Weight'.

Core strength

Oh dear 'Off the Bike Training' is not looking good so far is it? I seem to be completely against anything that does not involve training 'On the Bike'. Core strength however is in my opinion the one area of 'Off the Bike Training' that can be beneficial to TT and just about any other form of sport from Cycling to Ballroom Dancing and probably even Cheese Rolling!

Developing our core or trunk area is important for posture whilst riding a bike particularly in the TT position. It is proven that over much time, injuries related to posture are more likely for those with a weak core and poor posture. Such injuries may be prevented by developing core strength.

Working on the core also makes riding more efficient as it can increase stability in the saddle and even more importantly it can assist in the transfer of power through the kinetic chain that runs from the hands right through to the feet.

Developing core strength can also help with staying in the aerodynamic TT position for longer periods and reduce the backs tendency to over-arch, which in turn might improve power delivery through the pedals.

There is a whole array of core exercises and I have seen entire books and DVD's on the topic. However, in TT we are not particularly trying to build up too much muscle around the abdominals and I am a firm believer in keeping things simple. I therefore only carry out one simple core strength exercise called the 'Plank'. This exercise stresses the core muscles used in TT and therefore specific. I also have limited time to train and race TT and therefore don't want to spend loads of additional time or spending an entire evening doing lots of different core strengthening routines. I try to do 2 to 3 sets of 1 full minute in the plank position at the end of every training session when time allows. It is a good idea to do them at the end of a training session as your body will be already warmed up from the session and will only take a few minutes to execute.

Method:
Get into a push up position on the floor. Now bend your elbows 90 degrees and rest your weight on your forearms. Your elbows should be directly beneath and in line with shoulders and your body should remain in a straight line from your head to your heels. Feet should be at shoulder width apart.

Try to hold for one minute. Take a minute break and repeat 2–3 times. If you can manage more do so by all means. You might find that holding the position for a whole minute very hard to begin with. If this is the case, try to complete 30 second sets until you improve. If one minute becomes easy try 2 minutes. If 2 minutes becomes easy, lucky you and stop showing off!

UK Competition Records

It would be quite possible to display page after page of the UK competition records because there are just so many of them and the full set contains a lot of information. For this reason, I have omitted some of the records. Records I have not listed include those set by Teams, tandems, tricycles, team tricycles and tandem tricycles. I have also omitted the 12 and 24–hour TT records in this instance.

For simplicity I have chosen only to include records for individual men, ladies, juniors & juveniles for the most common distances of 10, 25, 50 and 100–mile distances.

Categories	Age in years
Men	18 and over
Ladies	18 and over
Juniors	16–18
Juveniles	12–16

10 Miles

category	name	club	year	time
Men	M Bialoblocki	One Pro Cycling	2016	16:35
Ladies	H Simmonds	Aerocoach	2016	18:36
Juniors	A Hartley	PH–MAS Cycling	2016	18:44
Juveniles	R Mullen	Planet X	2010	19:14

25 Miles

category	name	club	year	time
Men	M Bialoblocki	One Pro Cycling	2016	44:04
Ladies	H Simmonds	Aerocoach	2016	49:28
Juniors	M Langworthy	Mid Devon CC	2015	48:01
Juveniles	A Royle	Coveryourcar.co.uk RT	2009	50:22

50 Miles

category	name	club	year	time
Men	M. Bottrill	www.Drag2zero.com	2014	1:34:43
Ladies	H. Simmonds	Aerocoach	2016	1:42:20
Juniors	n/a			
Juveniles	n/a			

100 Miles

category	name	club	year	time
Men	A Duggleby	Vive le Velo	2017	3:16:51
Ladies	A Lethbridge	Drag2zero	2017	3:45:22
Juniors	n/a			
Juveniles	n/a			

Note: – Records to date at close of 2017 season. A full suite of records can be obtained from the Handbook which may be purchased from the organising body CTT.

World Hour Records

Welcome to the often confusing and misleading world of the Hour record. This record is for the longest distance travelled in kilometres on a bicycle over a period of one hour. There are many hour records including some extremely bizarre ones such as the record for riding a bicycle backwards. The most famous however is for upright bicycles meeting the requirements of the UCI and are attempted in a velodrome. The Hour record is one of the most prestigious in cycling and has attracted legendary riders such as Fausto Coppi, Jacques Anquetil, Miguel Indurain and of course the great Eddie Merckx.

The first recorded ride was in 1876 when the American Frank Dodds recorded a distance of 26.508km on his Penny Farthing. This record changed hands several times over the following decades and the current UCI unified record was set in June 2015 by Bradley Wiggins with a mark of 54.526km.

Whilst the attempt made by Wiggins is the new record, it is not the furthest distance recorded by the UCI under their regulations. Many earlier records including those set by British riders Graeme Obree & Chris Boardman were accepted by the UCI, but later derecognised following changes to the rules. Their records were later relegated to the category of 'Best Human Effort'.

For simplicity, I have provided the table below in the order of distance recorded instead of by date, and have highlighted the categories in which they relate with a prefix as follows: –

    (a)   UCI unified record (from 2014)
    (b)   UCI record (until 2014)
    (c)   UCI Best human effort

	Name	Velodrome Used	Date	Distance (km)
1	Chris Boardman (GBR)	Manchester (UK)	7/9/1996	56.375 (c)
2	Tony Rominger (SWI)	Du Lac, Bordeaux	5/11/1994	55.291 (c)
3	**Bradley Wiggins (GBR)**	**VeloPark London**	**7/6/2015**	**54.526 (a)**
4	Tony Rominger (SWI)	Du Lac, Bordeaux	22/10/1994	53.832 (c)
5	Miguel Indurain (ESP)	Du Lac, Bordeaux	2/9/1994	53.040 (c)
6	Alex Dowsett (GBR)	Manchester	2/5/2015	52.937 (a)
7	Graeme Obree (GBR)	Du Lac, Bordeaux	27/4/1994	52.713 (c)
8	Rohan Dennis (AUS)	Velodrome Suisse	8/2/2015	52.491 (a)

9	Chris Boardman (GBR)	Du Lac, Bordeaux	23/7/1993	52.270 (c)
10	Matthias Brandle (AUT)	Aigle, Switzerland	30/10/2014	51.852 (a)
11	Graeme Obree (GBR)	Hamar, Norway	17/7/1993	51.596 (c)
12	Francesco Moser (ITA)	Mexico City	23/1/1984	51.151 (c)
13	Jens Voigt (GER)	Grenchen, Switz	18/9/2014	51.115 (a)
14	Francesco Moser (ITA)	Mexico City	19/1/1984	50.808 (c)
15	Ondrej Sosenka (CZE)	Moscow, Russia	19/7/2005	49.700 (b)
16	Chris Boardman (GBR)	Manchester (UK)	27/10/2000	49.441 (b)
17	Eddy Merckx (BEL)	Mexico City	25/10/1972	49.431 (b)
18	Ole Ritter (DEN)	Mexico City	10/101968	48.653 (b)
19	Ferdi Bracke	Olympic	30/10/1967	48.093

	(BEL)	Velo, Rom		(b)
20	Roger Riviere (FRA)	Vigorelli, Milan	23/9/1959	47.347 (b)
21	Roger Riviere (FRA)	Vigorelli, Milan	10/9/1957	46.923 (b)
22	Ercole Baldini (ITA)	Vigorelli, Milan	19/9/1956	46.394 (b)
23	Jacques Anquetil (FRA)	Vigorelli, Milan	29/6/1956	46.159 (b)
24	Fausto Coppi (ITA)	Vigorelli, Milan	7/11/1942	45.798 (b)
25	Maurice Archambaud (FR)	Vigorelli, Milan	3/11/1937	45.767 (b)
26	Frans Slaats (NED)	Vigorelli, Milan	29/9/1937	45.485 (b)
27	Maurice Richard (FRA)	Vigorelli, Milan	14/10/1936	45.325 (b)
28	Giuseppe Olmo (ITA)	Vigorelli, Milan	31/10/1935	45.090 (b)
29	Maurice Richard (FRA)	Sint–Truiden, Belg	28/9/1933	44.777 (b)

30	Jan Van Hout (NED)	Roermond	25/8/1933	44.588 (b)
31	Oscar Egg (SWI)	Paris	18/8/1914	44.247 (b)
32	Marcel Berthet (FRA)	Paris	20/9/1913	43.775 (b)
33	Oscar Egg (SWI)	Paris	21/8/1913	43.525 (b)
34	Marcel Berthet (FRA)	Paris	7/8/1913	42.741 (b)
35	Oscar Egg (SWI)	Paris	22/8/1912	42.122 (b)
36	Marcel Berthet (FRA)	Paris	20/6/1907	41.520 (b)
37	Lucien Petit–Breton (FRA)	Paris	24/8/1905	41.110 (b)
38	Willie Hamilton (USA)	Colarado Spr US	3/7/1898	40.781
39	Oscar Van Den Eynde (B)	Vincennes, Paris	30/7/1897	39.240

40	Jules Dubois (FRA)	Buffalo, Paris	31/10/1894	38.220
41	Henri Desgrange (FRA)	Buffalo, Paris	11/5/1893	35.325
42	Frank Dodds (USA)	Cambridge Uni	25/8/1876	26.508

It should be noted that when the UCI grew concerned about the bikes being produced during the 1990's, they reset the record to Eddie Merckx's distance set in 1972 at the distance of 49.431km. The rules were also changed so that any attempts made should be done on a bike that resembled the bike Merckx used, meaning a standard steel frame with drop bars and wire spoke wheels. Chris Boardman broke that record in 2000 by only 10m and setting a new mark of 49.441km under those new rules. This was then beaten again by Czech rider Ondrej Sosenka in 2005 with a distance of 49.700km. Sosenka was also governed by the new rules and used a normal track bike. His machine was also noted for having a very heavy rear wheel.

In May 2014 the UCI decided to shift the rules once again in order to rekindle the interest in the hour record.

This meant that the use of a modern carbon fibre pursuit type bike with twin discs and TT bars would be allowed.

Jens Voigt was the first to attempt the record under these new rules and recorded a distance of 51.115km setting (or rather re-setting) the new unified record. The UCI rule change was clearly popular because very soon after Voigt's attempt, the world's top testers were queuing up to have a go. Matthias Brandle broke it just a month later and was the new holder until Rohan Dennis pushed the bar higher again a further 3 months later. British rider and TT specialist Alex Dowsett was next in queue and recorded a remarkable distance of 52.937km and bringing the title back to Great Britain. It was in June 2015 when world TT champion Bradley Wiggins of Great Britain made his attempt at the VeloPark, London. He smashed the record comfortably, putting it out of reach for most with a new mark of **54.526km.**

For me though the mark set by British rider Chris Boardman of 56.375km will remain the record as I firmly believe that the bike he used in 1996 was no better or advanced than the bike used by Bradley Wiggins during his 2015 record breaking ride. I am also a firm believer that the bikes used by the other, 'Best human effort' rides set by Moser, Obree, Indurain and Rominger, were also no more advanced than that ridden by the recent unified record holders. In fact, I would say that they might have even been disadvantaged considering the development of bikes today, but this is my opinion only.

They say that Boardmans mark of 56.375km is on too higher shelf and will never be beaten. However, they also said that about Eddie Merckx in 1972. Records are there to be broken and no doubt the UCI now have the formula right with a view to a whole wrath of the world's best testers fighting a new battle. Perhaps one of them will even beat Chris Boardman's distance one day and I can't wait to find out. Let the new battle for 'The Hour' commence!